BRIEF
INSIGHTS
ON MASTERING
THE BIBLE

Also by Michael S. Heiser

Brief Insights for Mastering Bible Study
Brief Insights for Mastering Bible Doctrine

BRIEF
INSIGHTS
ON MASTERING
THE BIBLE

80 Expert Insights,
Explained in a Single Minute

60-SECOND SCHOLAR SERIES

MICHAEL S. HEISER

ZONDERVAN

Brief Insights on Mastering the Bible
Copyright © 2018 by Michael S. Heiser

This title is also available as a Zondervan ebook.

Requests for information should be addressed to:
Zondervan, *3900 Sparks Dr. SE, Grand Rapids, Michigan 49546*

Library of Congress Cataloging-in-Publication Data

Names: Heiser, Michael S., author.
Title: Brief insights on mastering the Bible : 80 expert insights, explained in a
    single minute / Michael S. Heiser.
Description: Grand Rapids, MI : Zondervan, [2018] | Series: 60-second
    scholar series
Identifiers: LCCN 2017052849 | ISBN 9780310566601 (softcover)
Subjects: LCSH: Bible--Introductions.
Classification: LCC BS475.3 .H445 2018 | DDC 220.071--dc23 LC record
    available at https://lccn.loc.gov/2017052849

Cover design: Rick Szuecs Design
Cover art: www.flaticon.com
Interior design: Kait Lamphere

Printed in the United States of America

HB 11.01.2018

To my Bible college professors,
Doug Bookman, Ed Glenny, and Mike Stitzinger

CONTENTS

Part 3. Let the Biblical Writers
Do What They Did

Part 4. Let the First Five Books of
the Bible Be What They Are

Part 5. Let the Historical Books
Be What They Are

Part 6. Let the Prophetic Books
Be What They Are

Part 7. Let the Wisdom Books
Be What They Are

Part 8. Let the Gospels Be What They Are

Part 9. Let the Book of Acts Be What It Is

Part 10. Let the Epistles Be What They Are

Part 11. Let the Book of
Revelation Be What It Is

INTRODUCTION

The Best Piece of Advice
I Can Give You

This book is a collection of insights designed to help you understand the Bible. Since I'm a biblical scholar and professor with over twenty years of teaching experience, I've made a career of this sort of thing. There's a lot about the Bible that I think people should know. My own journey in Bible knowledge has convinced me there's one fundamental insight that, if faithfully observed, will help tremendously. It's the best piece of advice I can give you:

Let the Bible be what it is.

What do I mean? In simplest terms, I'm suggesting that the path to *real* biblical understanding requires that we don't make the Bible conform to denominational preferences. Don't filter the Bible through familiar traditions. Don't make it sound modern. Don't turn it into something it isn't. Just let it be what it is.

The insights I offer in this book are informed by the fundamental idea of letting the Bible be what it is. When we let the Bible be what it is, we can understand it as its original readers did—and as its writers did. I've applied this idea to the Bible and the people of the biblical world. Each chapter aims to provide insights for helping you understand Scripture.

Some of what you read will sound unfamiliar. Thousands of years separate us from the world of the Bible and the culture of the people God used to produce it. They weren't us; we aren't them. What they wrote is still important today, even vital, but we can only accurately discern the message if we let them speak as they spoke.

As a help to taking the Bible on its own terms—understanding it in its own contexts—I hope readers will avail themselves to my book *Brief Insights on Mastering Bible Study*. That resource will introduce readers to tools for moving past English translations and surface readings of the Bible. Some of the ideas introduced in this book are addressed in detail in my book *The Unseen World: Recovering the Supernatural Worldview of the Bible*.

In my experience, letting the Bible be what it is has not only made it more comprehensible but has also made it an endless fascination. I hope this book puts you on the same path.

PART 1

LET THE BIBLE BE WHAT IT IS

CHAPTER 1

Let the Bible Be What It Is

In the introduction, I told you that the best piece of advice for understanding the Bible I could give you was *let the Bible be what it is*. I need to unpack that statement a bit.

Letting the Bible be what it is means interpreting the Bible *in its own* context. Bible students talk a lot about interpreting the Bible in context. When most readers consider context, they think about the verses preceding and following whatever passage they happen to be looking at. Context involves much more.

There are many different contexts that, even today, dictate how we should understand what we read. For example, *the world in which we live* provides a context. If I wrote the word "text" on a blackboard (or whiteboard) today in a room full of college students and asked what the word means, I would hear very different answers than I would have heard twenty years ago. Students today would immediately think of a wireless, electronic message. Their worldview is dominated by technology. That wouldn't have been true a few decades ago. That was a different world.

The type of writing or document dictates how we should understand what's written. In literary terms, this refers to genre. If I was looking at the word "court" in a legal document, I'd interpret the word much differently than if I was holding a tennis magazine. The word "treat" in a doctor's note means something different than it would if you found it on a grocery list. Genre is a context that is crucial for interpretation.

There are many other examples. Your culture, religious thinking, political system, family unit, and social structure all influence how you processes the Bible. We might know that intellectually, but we often fail to embrace the fact that the biblical writers wrote for their immediate audience, who had contexts quite different than our own.

Interpreting the Bible in context means interpreting it in light of the worldview in which it was produced. Filtering the Bible through our worldview or any worldview that came after the biblical period means altering how the Bible was originally meant to be read. We need to let the Bible be what it is—an ancient work from another time and place. To apply the Bible to our lives accurately, we need to know what it actually teaches.

CHAPTER 2

Don't Second-Guess God's Decisions in Inspiration

I n my experience, some Bible students are concerned that the worldview disconnection between us and the ancient biblical writers means that the Bible can't speak to issues of our time. That isn't the case. While the Bible is a premodern and prescientific book, the truths it asserts are timeless.

We need to trust God's wisdom in inspiration. If God had wanted to inspire Scripture in a modern age, he could have done so. It was God who decided to prepare men living between the second millennium BC and the first century AD to produce the books of the Bible. It was God who decided that they were ready for the task, despite cultural attitudes that we would deem backward. It was God who didn't require the writers to have advanced scientific and technological knowledge to write everlasting truth. These were God's choices.

God's choices were good choices. God is not incompetent. God intended Scripture to be applicable to people who would live well beyond the first century. He also intended Scripture to be understood by the people who received it originally. Since God is omniscient, he could have given writers living thousands of years ago advanced knowledge without their knowing it. But that knowledge could not have been understood by anyone reading the text until millennia later. Millions of people living prior to our time would have had no hope of understanding their Bible. That would have defeated the communicative purpose of the Bible. The "whole counsel of God" (Acts 20:27) would not have been comprehensible, which undermines inspiration's purpose (2 Tim. 3:17).

God in his wisdom prepared ancient people to express truths that are independent of the knowledge base of one particular time. Ancient people were entirely capable of communicating fundamentally significant ideas that are absolutely relevant today—that God is creator, that people were created in his image, that human life is sacred, that people cannot provide their own salvation from sin, that there is good and evil, and so on.

As we'll see later, this perspective is important for understanding what the Bible says in certain places. It's also critical for apologetics. Hostile critics of Scripture often belittle it for being premodern. But this criticism only has weight if the Bible was intended to contain modern knowledge but falls short. Nothing about inspiration presumes this, and so the criticism amounts to being angry with the Bible for not being what it was never intended to be. That's deeply flawed logic. But we play into the hands of the antagonist when we try to make the Bible something it isn't. We must honor God's wise choice to inspire it in the time and place he did.

CHAPTER 3

Inspiration Was a Process, Not an Event

Because the Bible quite clearly calls itself "God-breathed" (2 Tim. 3:16), we tend to think about inspiration as an otherworldly event. That's a misconception. The Bible is a divine book, given what 2 Timothy 3:16 says, but it's also a thoroughly human book. Failing to grasp its humanness can lead to all sorts of problems in understanding it and can even cause doubt about its authenticity. Embracing the humanity of the Bible is enormously helpful for understanding what's in the Bible and why it says the things it does.

For example, we have four Gospels. Three of them (Matthew, Mark, and Luke) overlap in content a lot of the time with respect to what they include about the life of Jesus. But they often have things in different order. Dialogue isn't always the same. Certain details of episodes in the life of Jesus might be in two accounts and missing in the third. And when it comes to the Gospel of John, 90 percent (literally) of what's in that Gospel isn't in the other three.

One thing for sure *isn't* part of the explanation: the notion that the words dropped from heaven or were downloaded into the brains of the Gospel writers. The notion that God handed out every word just doesn't work with the Gospels. The Bible never describes inspiration that way. It does describe very human acts. Writers record events and thoughts. They build arguments. They express themselves in poetry. They use sources. They create links between their work and other parts of Scripture.

Writing involves work and careful thought. Biblical books were not slapped together. The Bible bears the marks of human decision making on every page and in every paragraph. Biblical literature follows the conventions of the day for competent, professional writing. Authors are sensitive to genre, structure, literary devices, word choice, poetic parallelism, and narrative art. No part of any biblical book just "happened."

God chose a wide range of people and providentially prepared them for the moment he would prompt them, either by his Spirit or by someone else's influence, to write something for the posterity of God's people. God put them in situations that would lead them to write the message God wanted preserved. He didn't need to put them into a trance or control their hands like we do to little children who are learning their letters. They were his instruments, not his puppets.

CHAPTER 4

Inspiration Wasn't a Paranormal Experience

Christians believe the Bible is inspired. We intuitively presume that means that God was involved in producing Scripture. But how exactly did that happen?

In my experience, explanations of inspiration can get pretty strange. I regularly had students in Bible college think of inspiration as some sort of episode where the Holy Spirit took control of the human author. I've heard pastors and Bible teachers talk about God controlling the hand, fingers, and even the mind of the writer. That sounds more like an episode of *The X-Files* or *Fringe* than biblical theology.

What do I mean? The prophet Isaiah wasn't busy making breakfast one morning when he was suddenly cast by the Spirit of God into a mindless, catatonic state. The words of the book that bears his name weren't downloaded into his brain. His body didn't stiffen as though possessed, save for one arm, that unbeknownst to him was busy filling a scroll with words from God. Isaiah wouldn't have later marveled at the result, eager to find out what he'd just written while zombified. This is the sort of portrayal one encounters in occult literature or descriptions of what psychics call automatic writing. The Bible describes nothing like this. Inspiration wasn't a paranormal event.

We know inspiration didn't work this way from the Bible itself. True, the Bible does say that its content is "God-breathed," but that's just a statement about its ultimate source. The Bible bears the marks of human thought, skill, and decision on every page.

According to Scripture, Scripture is both divine and human (2 Peter 1:16–21). The authors didn't write independently of God's influence and providence, but they did indeed write what we have in the Bible. The biblical writers at times tell us directly that they had a purpose or agenda for what they did (John 20:30–31; 1 Cor. 4:14; 2 Cor. 13:10). Even when God commanded something to be written down, Scripture doesn't describe the person commanded as losing control of their minds and becoming unthinking robots (Ex. 17:14; Num. 5:23; Deut. 31:19, 30).

We therefore shouldn't expect that God had to whisper the words of the Bible into the ear of the writer. The inspiration of Scripture was the culmination of a long process involving many dedicated hands. The biblical writers—named or not—were God's instruments because he providentially prepared and used them in the task. God didn't need mind control. They did the job, God guided the result, and we are the beneficiaries.

CHAPTER 5

Editing Was Part of the Process of Biblical Inspiration

I f you're like most people in the developed world (so it seems), you talk about yourself and your family using social media. If you're the exception rather than the rule, social media is still understandable by analogy—it's like a personal diary of what you, your friends, and your family encounter and do every day.

We know how something like that is supposed to read. It would be written in the first person: *I* did this, then *we* did that. How odd would it sound if you were reading a friend's Facebook page and they talked about themselves using the third person? Instead of what you'd expect your friend to post ("I went to a movie last night"), your friend talked about herself as though she were someone else ("She went to a movie last night"). When someone writes about themselves you expect the first person, not the third. It's because of that expectation that scholars can tell biblical books were edited.

One of the best examples of this is the first four verses of the book of Ezekiel:

In the thirtieth year, in the fourth month, on the fifth day of the month, as *I was among* the exiles by the Chebar canal, the heavens were opened, and *I saw* visions of God. On the fifth day of the month (it was the fifth year of the exile of

King Jehoiachin), the word of the LORD came **to Ezekiel** the priest, the son of Buzi, in the land of the Chaldeans by the Chebar canal, and the hand of the LORD was **upon him** there. As *I looked*, behold, a stormy wind came out of the north.

The first verse uses the first person. I italicized two examples. The beginning creates the expectation that Ezekiel is writing about himself. But in verse three there is a switch to the third person (boldface). Now the writer is clearly not Ezekiel, but is an anonymous author referring to Ezekiel in the third person. Verse four switches *back* to first person.

These switches are the telltale signs of an editor. The book of Ezekiel has many such instances, as do many other biblical books. That we don't know the identity of these editors is of little consequence, since the authors of many books in the Bible (particularly the Old Testament) are unknown.

Knowing that biblical books were edited helps us address issues in the text where something appears misplaced. These are not errors but telegraph something to the reader. Scholars work at discerning the purpose of such things. Understanding editing can also help us put certain statements in the Bible in the right chronological context for interpretation.

CHAPTER 6

The Bible Is Not an Exhaustive Repository of All Truth

One of life's great ironies is that we all believe things that are demonstrably false, and perhaps downright silly. Otherwise intelligent people really did believe that the Mayan calendar foretold the end of the world. Some people believe that we never went to the moon. And who knows how many people now believe the earth is really flat?

The Bible is no exception to ill-founded beliefs. One of the most obviously wrong is the notion that the Bible is the fount of all knowledge—that every single truth is found within its pages. That's nonsense. So is its correlating thought: that if something isn't mentioned in the Bible, it *isn't* true.

The truth of my assertions can be demonstrated thousands of times over. The Bible makes no mention of cars, microwave ovens, toilet paper, planets beyond Saturn, bubble gum, coffee, smart phones, electricity, and disposable diapers. And yet it's true that all of them are real. The idea that everything true is found in the Bible is simply false. And yet I've heard Christians say it more than once, even from the pulpit.

One problem with such thinking (and there are many) is that those who think rejecting these ideas is a denial of inspiration tend to force the Bible to comment on things of which it has nothing to say. The result is ill-informed "Bible teaching" that is patently bizarre.

For example, some people will insist that the Bible mentions dinosaurs, countries like China, races within humanity, or flying saucers. The Bible says nothing about these things. Leviathan is not a dinosaur. It is a well-known ancient symbol for chaos and disorder outside as well as within the Bible. The Table of Nations includes only countries in the ancient Near East and Mediterranean. The subject of biological race distinction was unknown to biblical writers, who primarily separated peoples according to religion and language. People groups in the Bible are distinguished by language, geography, and the gods they worship. Ezekiel 1 does not describe a UFO—all the imagery in that passage is known from ancient art and sculpture.

Forcing the Bible to "teach" something absent from its pages means distorting its content and producing false beliefs in the name of truth. This is not only irresponsible, but it also sets up the Bible to fail as a source of truth for the things it does talk about.

The solution is simple. We need to let the Bible be what it is. Its content is deliberately selective since each author, living and writing under God's providence, had goals for communication. Our task as Bible interpreters is to understand what Scripture says in its own context, not to add to it.

CHAPTER 7

Most of the Authors of Biblical Books Are Unknown

It goes without saying that understanding a book requires knowing who wrote it. This is especially true of nonfiction, where the author's background, political and religious views, and education help frame what we're reading. Unfortunately, few ancient books, including the books of the Bible, specifically name their author.

Most of the authorship problem as it relates to the Bible concerns the Old Testament. For example, we have no idea who wrote books like Judges, 1–2 Kings, and 1–2 Chronicles. Those books never name an author. Even books that bear the names of people are uncertain—for the same reason. The books of 1–2 Samuel never claim that Samuel wrote them. The same goes for Ruth, Esther, and Joshua.

Some Old Testament books have partially known authorship, but that means that parts are problematic. Psalms is a good example. The psalms' superscriptions were likely added long after the psalms were composed, so they aren't reliable indicators. Phrases like "Psalm of David" are actually inconclusive since the Hebrew phrase (*le-dawid*) can mean "by David," "for David," or "about David."

The New Testament is less anonymous. The author of the book of Hebrews is unknown. Scholars argue about a few of the books that claim authorship (e.g., 1–2 Peter), but arguments contesting

Peter's authorship are not at all conclusive. Since there are more than one James and John associated with the life of Jesus, there is some degree of ambiguity for books bearing those names.

Because authorship is uncertain, it is best in interpretation never to base an interpretation on a presumed author. Guessing at an author and then presuming that person's background as part of interpretation is a shaky strategy.

Because of this lack of clarity, scholars have had to work hard to find clues in the books themselves that situate them in the flow of biblical history. Things like allusions to events outside Israel (e.g., a battle), an environmental catastrophe (e.g., a famine), or even a natural disaster (e.g., an earthquake) are important clues.

Even without an author, if scholars can situate a book in a specific historical context, that book can be coherently interpreted. For this reason, whenever you study a book of the Bible, it's wise to read a serious academic introduction to it that deals with authorship, setting, and questions of circumstance. You can't assume that you know how to situate a book just by its title.

CHAPTER 8

The Bible Is a Product of Its Time

S aying the Bible is a product of its times takes us into the tricky (and, for most, mind-numbing) subject of biblical chronology. Taking the Bible on its own terms means coming to grips with the fact that biblical writers were influenced by current and past events.

The content of the Bible ostensibly spans from creation to the end of time as we know it, but that's not really what I'm talking about. I'm referring to the chronological boundaries for the writing of the Bible—the times in which its authors and editors lived. In round numbers, if one presumes Moses had a hand in writing any part (or all) of the Torah, the beginning of biblical composition would have occurred in roughly 1450 BC. The last book of the Bible, the book of Revelation, would have been composed around AD 100. That's roughly a 1,500-year span.

What was going on in that span? How do we get these numbers? Those questions are related. The Bible doesn't provide us with "real time" dating of events. In other words, it doesn't tell us explicitly that an Old Testament event occurred 700 years before Christ, or that Paul wrote something three decades after the resurrection. The Bible instead gives us relative chronology—what happened before or after what. In addition, the Bible doesn't date events by astronomical events—the way true real-time chronology must be calculated, since time is measured by the motion of earth around the sun and the appearance of the moon and stars in relation to the earth's own spin.

Absolute chronology—actual numerical dates—is assigned to biblical events on the basis of synchronisms between people and events in the Bible that can be correlated with the records of another ancient civilization that *did* keep time by astronomy. Thousands of such records have survived—tables of lunar cycles and celestial observations that modern astronomers can reproduce to align ancient records with actual time. When something in the Bible correlates to those ancient records, we can fix the Bible in real time.

Correlations have a progressively high degree of accuracy and certainty moving from about 1000 BC forward. Events earlier than 1000 BC have less certainty because astronomical records are fewer and less consistent. There's also simply less chronological material from places like Mesopotamia and Egypt for reconstructing their own history. There are gaps, for example, in the lists of kings and the number of years they reigned.

Situating the Bible in real time allows biblical scholars to know how events in the Bible align with events in Egypt, Assyria, Babylon, Greece, Rome, and other civilizations. Political upheaval, droughts, famines, wars, and natural disasters sometimes become factors in what biblical writers say and why they say it. *Time* is therefore an important context for taking the Bible on its own terms. We should not neglect it.

CHAPTER 9

The Setting of a Biblical Story Wasn't Necessarily the Time at Which It Was Written

Most of us who read the Bible with regularity consider its contents factually true. Because that's the case, many readers are prone to assume that what they're reading was written at the same time as the events described, or at least very close to the time of those events. Sometimes that assumption isn't far from the reality, but in many instances, that isn't the case.

For example, most scholars would place the earliest of the four Gospels within a few decades of Jesus's life. The reason for that gap in time is clear from a close reading of the New Testament. The apostles thought that the Lord's return was imminent (Rom. 13:11; 1 Peter 4:7; James 5:8; Heb. 10:25–27). When it became apparent that Jesus might not return in their lifetimes, there was a sense of urgency to put what they had experienced and heard during their time with Jesus into writing for posterity.

As it turned out, the entirety of the New Testament was written by roughly AD 100, just over a half century after the death and resurrection of Jesus. In comparison to other historical works of the ancient world, that's a short span of time. According to the chronology that can be gleaned from the book of Acts, the epistles were written within a few months or years of Paul's ministry in the congregations to which they were written.

When it comes to the Old Testament, things are different. Even if we presume Moses recorded the lives of the patriarchs in Genesis, he would have been writing several centuries after the fact. Many Old Testament books have unknown authors, which makes it difficult to align their events and their authorship. As we'll see in later chapters, the books that detail Israel's story from the exodus to the monarchy (e.g., Exodus, Deuteronomy, and Joshua through 2 Kings) contain evidence that they were written several centuries after the events they describe.

The gaps between the event and its recording are no reason to assume inaccuracy. External sources and disciplines such as archaeology show that the contents of these books are coherent and in concert with the times they portray. Ancient societies had strong oral historical traditions. Present day historians who study oral cultures tell us that the people of these cultures can memorize prodigious amounts of material with exactitude. Modern cultures that adopt writing have no need for this discipline. So despite our unfamiliarity with oral history, it would have been commonplace in distant antiquity. Finally, the fact that parts of Israel's history hadn't yet been written in a *book* doesn't mean that it wasn't written elsewhere. We know Old Testament writers had sources. The absence of one doesn't require the absence of the other.

When it comes to understanding Scripture, we need to educate ourselves on both timelines—the events portrayed and the time of writing. Understanding both will help us recover the perspective of both the biblical characters and the writers.

CHAPTER 10

Everything in the Bible
Isn't about Jesus

I f you've been a Christian for very long or were raised in a Christian church, chances are that you've heard that the Bible is really about Jesus. That cliché has some truth to it, but it's misleading.

The truth is that there's a lot in the Bible that isn't about Jesus. Procedures for diagnosing and treating leprosy (Lev. 13:1–14:57) aren't about Jesus. Laws forbidding people who've had sex or lost blood (Lev. 15) from entering sacred space aren't about Jesus. The spiritual, social, and moral corruption in the days of the Judges (Judg. 17–21) wasn't put in the Bible to tell us about Jesus. The Tower of Babel incident (Gen. 11:1–9) doesn't point us to Jesus. When Ezra commanded Jews who'd returned from exile to divorce the gentile women they'd married (Ezra 9–10), he wasn't foreshadowing anything about Jesus.

The point is straightforward: No Israelite would have thought of a messianic deliverer when reading these or many other passages. And no New Testament writer alludes to them to explain who Jesus was or what he said.

So why is this idea so prevalent?

In my experience, the prevailing motivation seems to be offered to encourage people to read their Bibles. That's a good incentive. But it may also serve as an excuse to avoid the hard work of figuring out what's really going on in many passages. People are taught to extrapolate what they read to some point of connection with the life and ministry of Jesus—no matter how foreign to Jesus the passage appears. Imagination isn't a good method for interpreting the Bible. Not only does it lack boundaries that prevent flawed interpretations, and even heresies, but it makes Scripture serve our ability to be clever.

Recognizing the inaccuracy of this assumption is important for a few simple but important reasons. First, if we filter passages that aren't about Jesus through something Jesus did and said, we can't hope to understand what those passages are actually about and why God had them in the Bible in the first place. Second, the assumption can lead to minimizing or ignoring passages in which we can't clearly see Jesus. When Jesus isn't "clear" in a given passage, and we've been taught that it's somehow about him, it's easy to just give up and let pastors and others tell us what they "see." Every passage in the Bible is there for a reason. If we want to understand Scripture, we need to let it be what it is and discover its true context.

PART 2

LET THE ANCIENT ISRAELITES BE WHO THEY WERE

CHAPTER 11

The World Known to the Biblical Writers Was a Lot Smaller than Ours

Genesis 10 is known to Bible scholars as the "Table of Nations." The chapter is a biblical explanation of what happened in the centuries after Noah and his family disembarked the ark, having survived the flood. The Table of Nations describes how the descendants of Noah's three sons—Shem, Ham, and Japheth— repopulated the earth, forming the nations known in the rest of the Old Testament story. In terms of the unfolding narrative of Genesis, the chapter is a precursor to the Tower of Babel story (Gen. 11:1–9), where the nations were divided and dispersed by God.

There's an obvious problem with the Table of Nations—or for those who let the Bible be what it is, an obvious disconnect between the world of the biblical writers and the world we know today. The Table of Nations shows no knowledge whatsoever of the geography belonging to North America, South America, Australia, China, India, and Scandinavia. The same is true of the knowledge of earth's geography in the New Testament (cf. Acts 2). The known world in biblical times covered a fraction of the size of the globe we know today.

This is no surprise if we let the Bible be what it is. The biblical "world" is composed of seventy nations that are situated in what we now call the ancient Near East (or modern Middle East) on the land masses that surround the Mediterranean Sea. There is no hint in the Scriptures of any land mass beyond this region.

We can learn a lesson from other's misguided attempts to make the Bible into something it isn't with respect to the true size of the world. Once Europeans achieved the ability to cross the Atlantic and circumnavigate the world, people immediately questioned where these other countries and people came from. Most Europeans, well familiar with the Bible, presumed these people must have come from Adam. But how did the descendants of Noah produce these peoples?

All sorts of strange proposals were offered in answer to these questions. Those efforts in turn produced theories of race, including the theory that non-European (nonwhite) races came from sub-humans or humans separate from and inferior to Adam. The rest is history. Europeans believed that embracing these explanations, which are inherently flawed and racist, was necessary to preserve biblical authority. Despite their absence in the Table of Nations, the Bible *had* to speak to the discovery of these new lands and peoples. These interpretive gymnastics institutionalized racial ideas that the Bible never endorses.

CHAPTER 12

Biblical Writers Believed That God Made the World They Knew, Not the World They Didn't Know

The biblical writers didn't know a lot of things we know today. That's especially true when it comes to areas like medicine, engineering, and science. Today, many Christians want to make the Bible a source of science due to the perceived threat of evolution. Other Bible believers try to force certain passages into teaching evolutionary theory. But the biblical writers had no concept of a theory that was formulated in the nineteenth century. Both approaches are flawed and don't allow the Bible to be what it is.

The biblical authors were premodern and therefore prescientific in the modern sense. The Bible itself informs us of this in some transparent ways. For example, ancient Israelites believed the seat of emotions and decision-making was the internal organs (heart, intestines, kidneys; see Ps. 16:7; 26:2; 31:9; Prov. 20:27; Jer. 11:20; Rev. 2:23). We use such language today metaphorically because we know that emotions are brain-based. Biblical Hebrew doesn't even have a word for "brain."

Hebrews 7:4–10 mentions that the descendants of Levi existed in the loins of Abraham. We know from modern science that a person's full genetics result from conception, an insight into procreation of which the author of Hebrews would have had no concept.

Biblical cosmology is also prescientific. For example, many interpreters see in Old Testament passages a three-tiered universe: heavens above, earth beneath, and water under the earth (Ex. 20:4; Phil. 2:10; Rev. 5:3). This perspective would have been common throughout the ancient Near East and Mediterranean.

The biblical writers had no intention (or ability) to teach modern science in Genesis or any other passage. They put forth ideas that transcend the facts of biology, physics, chemistry, and any other hard science: God created the world and everything in it. This assertion does not contradict science, though many scientists want to resist it. God in his wisdom gave us a truth proposition that surpasses scientific theories and debates. Let critics deride the Bible for not being what it wasn't intended to be—they will sound hopelessly foolish.

CHAPTER 13

Ancient Israelite Culture Didn't Drop from Heaven

People hostile to the Bible often attack it on the basis of the cultural customs found in its pages. For example, critics find easy targets in the Bible's patriarchal culture, attitudes toward slavery, and social standards. But in criticizing these customs, they make the fundamental mistake of not letting the Bible be what it is.

If we believe—and the Bible is very plain in this regard—that God chose the time, place, and people to prompt the writing of what we call the Bible, then the notion that God invented or inspired their culture is nonsense. *They already had a culture—with many elements common to the wider world of the ancient Near East and Mediterranean.*

What we see in Scripture is that the Bible presupposes culture. Biblical laws, for instance, presume polygamy (Deut. 21:15–17), yet the Bible doesn't require it (in fact, its portrayals are negative). There are laws regarding slavery (Ex. 21), but there is no record that God installed the institution as something desirable or sanctified.

In other words, cultural institutions that we find offensive today (and rightly so) were part of the culture of the people God prompted to write Scripture. God didn't first create their culture, nor did he insist they change their culture before using them to produce the books of the Bible. God knew what he was getting when he called Semitic people living 3,000 years ago to write Scripture. God was not the author of their culture. Only in the cases where practices are tied to Israel's worship (e.g., their religious calendar) can God be viewed as an instigator.

In some fundamental respects, culture was incidental to God's plans. God gave Israel a body of wisdom literature that laid out broad principles of justice and mercy that transcend all cultures. He kept reminding Israelites through the prophets that people from all nations would come to recognize him as the true God and therefore be members of God's family.

This latter point has another aspect to it. God knew that his people would eventually encompass people from every nation. The point is simple but profound: *the people of God are independent of culture—their identity is not bound to a single cultural expression.* This is by design.

It makes little sense then for believers to presume that cultural practices in the Bible are something to be imitated for theological purposes. It is equally fallacious for critics of the Bible to pretend that the Bible can be criticized for culture. Our focus ought to be on the truth claims of the Bible that transcend culture.

CHAPTER 14

Biblical People Embraced the Idea of an Active Supernatural World

What would you think if a Christian friend confided in you that they believed they had been helped by a guardian angel? Would you expect that there was actually a more rational explanation? What if one of your kids told you about a dream they had the previous night where Jesus told them to tell you to call 911 because the elderly neighbor next door was lying on the floor unconscious? Would you go and see?

Because we live in a modern world, many of us are prone to doubt such things. We know that ancient people who lack modern scientific concepts incorrectly attribute natural things to the actions of spiritual beings. Weather is a good example. There are sound scientific reasons why droughts and floods occur, and why it rains and doesn't rain. We feel no need to attribute these things directly to the hand of God, although we look for his providence in the circumstances of such events.

The Bible clearly teaches that angels, demons, and Satan are personal, spiritual entities. As we'll see in other essays, those sorts of spiritual beings are not the only ones the Bible talks about. The Bible talks about several spiritual beings that interact with humanity and view the earth as their dominion.

In my experience, while Christians enthusiastically embrace

their belief in the Trinity, they are far more cautious with the rest of the supernatural world. Even though most would say they believe in angels, the idea of angels genuinely interacting with us loses some support. The dark side is held at an even greater distance. Do we believe that demon possession is real? Many people today, including many Christians, consider demon possession to be a misdiagnosis of a psychiatric problem. Perhaps we might think that biblical people didn't understand psychological disorders.

And then there are the "weird" passages that deal with the unseen world. Do we really believe that the angels who sinned (Gen. 6:1–4) are being held hostage by God until the end times (2 Peter 2:4–5; Jude 6; Rev. 9)? Do we believe that people can contact the dead or other spiritual beings (1 Sam. 28:1–19)? How would the Old Testament prohibitions (Deut. 18:9–14) against doing these sorts of things make sense if they weren't possible?

People living in biblical times would have had no such intellectual struggles. They were predisposed to believing in an animate supernatural world that regularly intersected with their own. Is it possible that our modern Christian subcultures have trained us to think that our theology *precludes* these sorts of experiences? If we want to understand Scripture, we cannot think like modern skeptics.

CHAPTER 15

Most People in the Biblical World Had Never Read the Bible

This might seem like a shocking statement. It's one of the more dramatic examples of how our lives as Christians are quite unlike the lives of biblical people. But once you give the assertion some thought, it becomes clear that it's true.

The Bible was written in stages. The Old Testament wasn't complete until the fifth century BC, roughly a thousand years *after* the exodus of Israel from Egypt. And even in the best scenario, after completion there would have only been *one* Bible for decades. Everything had to be copied by hand.

During the Old Testament period leading up to the exile (sixth century BC), the emphasis in Israel's faith was the temple, its rituals, and the sacred calendar of holy days. Not only was there no complete Bible, but even the books that existed were the property of the temple and its priests. The average Israelite only read or heard snippets from it, such as the *Shema*, Israel's creed (Deut. 6:4) or some of God's commands. The Torah commanded people to "write them on the doorposts of your house and on your gates" (Deut. 6:9).

There were no synagogues in ancient Israel either. The synagogue came about during the exile after the temple was destroyed. Israelite priests could not possibly teach everyone house-to-house, as they had other assigned duties and the population was too large.

For most of the Old Testament period, people learned biblical content from storytelling and from their parents (Deut. 6:7).

In New Testament times, things got a little better. Jews had their Bible, the Old Testament. It would have been very rare for someone to have a Torah at home due to the expense and labor of hand-copying. But chances were high you were exposed to more of the Old Testament through regular attendance at the synagogue than ever before.

The Old Testament (in Greek) would have been the Bible of the early Christians. The New Testament books were written in the first century AD between the late 40s and 100. But most of those were letters sent to individual churches. A church would have to copy the letter and send it to another church, where it would be read aloud. It also took a couple centuries for early Christians, led by the Spirit, to discern which of these new writings should be considered sacred, on par with the Scriptures they had inherited from Israel.

All of this leads to the fact that most biblical people were profoundly ignorant of what we think of today as the Bible. Most were not "having devotions" and "studying the Word." We ought to be careful when criticizing something they said or did, as though they knew better. They may not have. We have something they didn't—and so we are more accountable.

PART 3

LET THE BIBLICAL WRITERS DO WHAT THEY DID

CHAPTER 16

The Biblical Writers Were Not Semiliterate Amateurs

I have several friends who write professionally. Some write resumes for people. Others write fiction or for newspapers. Several are bloggers or freelancers. Any writing trade requires a certain skill set—and that means more than having a firm grasp of grammar, spelling, and punctuation.

There are several overlooked aspects of writing as a trade. For example, knowing your audience and their expectations is crucial. Audiences naturally expect clarity and readable prose. But there's a part of audience expectation that is less familiar. The competence of a writer is also judged by whether a writer produces content in the expected form. Those expectations arise from the *type* of document in view—its genre.

All of us take the form of a document for granted. We don't even think about it unless we encounter a flawed example. If you were in court, for example, and your lawyer handed a judge a document only to have the judge growl out loud that the document wasn't prepared according to required specifications, you'd wonder if your lawyer knew what he or she was doing. If you picked up a book that had the table of contents in the back, you'd think immediately that the publisher or the writer was incompetent. If you were reading the first chapter of a novel that told you how the story was going to end, you'd wonder if the author had any sense of plot. Every genre includes expectations about the right way to write.

When writers violate this sense of convention, most readers would think that the writer is an inexperienced amateur—a *hack*, in literary terms. The biblical writers were not hacks.

The Bible is filled with all types of literature: laws, legal cases, treaties, poetry, historical narrative, apocalyptic visions, letters, annals, parables, and speeches are examples. Each one came with expectations of how that particular type of literature "ought" to be written and structured. The fact that biblical material has a high degree of conformity to ancient examples of all these literary genres shows us that the people who wrote Scripture knew what they were doing. They were competent writers. The Bible wasn't the result of amateur hour.

This has two implications for us as Bible students. First, we're obligated to discover what the biblical writers were doing. We need to learn something about the literary genres of the Bible and how biblical writers wrote according to such forms. Second, we need to let our knowledge of what the biblical writers were doing dictate our reading. Simplistic readings of the Bible that are inattentive to what the biblical writers were doing—and why—will not produce an accurate interpretation. Part of understanding the Bible is understanding each writer's craft.

CHAPTER 17

The Writers of the Bible Structured What They Wrote to Convey Meaning

If you've ever had to outline a paper or prepare notes for a company meeting at work, you know that how the elements in your writing or presentation are arranged will matter a lot for how it's received and understood.

How information is "packaged" can be crucial for comprehension. People who work with large amounts of data know especially well that their information's presentation often dictates whether their work is grasped or ignored. For that reason, pollsters and statisticians often use visuals—infographics, pie charts, tables—to present their work. A good visual can draw the eye immediately to the most important points the data conveys.

When it comes to writing, skilled authors structure material for the same pay-off. They may not use colorful graphs, but there are ways of structuring material to draw the eye—or, in the case of the ancient world, the ear—to the important points.

One example that's well known to biblical scholars is the use of *chiasm*. The word *chiasm* is derived from the Greek letter *chi*, which is written like the letter X. Imagine cutting the X vertically in half. The arms of an X move toward the center point and then veer outward again in an opposite direction. Chiasm refers to doing that in writing. The writer builds a scene or an argument in one direction and then begins to "work backward" following the same path.

By way of illustration, consider Romans 2:6–11. Notice how the content of the verses moves toward a point (marked by letters) and then "reverses" itself element-by-element:

A. God will judge everyone equitably (v. 6).
 B. Those who seek God's glory and honor will receive eternal life (v. 7).
  C. Those who are unrighteous will receive judgment (v. 8).
  C'. Those who are unrighteous will suffer judgment (v. 9).
 B'. The righteous receive glory and honor (v. 10).
A'. God will judge everyone without partiality (v. 11).

The arrangement is deliberate, not accidental. Like the rest of the letters of the New Testament (the Epistles), Romans would have been read aloud. Alert listeners would have detected repetition patterns like this structure. They would have made the content easier to remember. And like this example, the structuring highlights the most important thoughts in a pattern.

Biblical writers wrote with *intention*. We need to read them that way.

CHAPTER 18

The Biblical Writers Did Their Homework

Most people are familiar with how libraries divide books into fiction and nonfiction. The difference, of course, is that fiction is contrived—it's storytelling where the story is an exercise of the imagination. This is true even if the story is based on real events and people. If the story did not actually happen, then no matter how closely it resembles reality, it's still fiction. Nonfiction, in simplest terms, is the opposite. The writer is giving the reader a recounting of something that actually happened or providing information that is factually real.

We don't often think about it, but there are many subcategories to both classifications. Not all nonfiction is created equal. Some of it is academic: the writer did a good deal of research, and the research is detailed and dense.

The biblical writers were careful researchers as well. Scholars know that for two reasons. First, the Scripture itself informs us that sources were used for points of information. A "Book of Jashar" is mentioned as a source for biblical material on two occasions (Josh. 10:13; 2 Sam. 1:18). Numbers 21:14 refers to a source called "The Book of the Wars of the Lord." Luke, who was not an eyewitness to the life of Jesus, apparently made use of sources in writing his Gospel (Luke 1:1–4).

Second, even when the biblical writers don't name their sources, scholars have been able to trace phrases, poetic lines, and symbols found in Scripture to older or contemporary sources in the writings of other civilizations. Biblical writers were under no obligation to indicate when they used sources. There was no sense of intellectual property in the ancient world that required anything like modern footnoting. Luke and Paul quoted classical Greek poets on several occasions (Epimenides of Crete in Acts 17:28; Menander in 1 Cor. 15:33; Epimenides of Crete in Titus 1:12). The author of Psalm 74 draws material from the Canaanite Baal Cycle about the defeat of the primeval sea, which is personified as a sea beast (Leviathan) to describe how God brought order out of chaos. Portions of Proverbs 22 are drawn from an earlier Egyptian text called "The Wisdom of Amenemope."

Inspiration does not forbid the use of sources. In fact, the use of sources is another illustration of how inspiration was not a paranormal experience. Biblical writers used material known in their day for factual information and to help articulate arguments and theological assertions. We do the same sort of thing today when we use information outside the Bible to help people understand Scripture. The difference, of course, is that what we say isn't divine revelation.

CHAPTER 19

The Biblical Writers Were Literary Artists

Most of us can remember taking a course in high school or college about English literature. In my experience, that was the course where I was first introduced to techniques used by writers beyond straightforward prose sentences. To be blunt, there are reasons why Shakespeare doesn't sound like the newspaper. Fine literature like Shakespeare—and the Bible—is what it is because of deliberate techniques and strategies used by the writer.

The biblical writers use an amazing array of literary techniques. Some are familiar to us, like similes and metaphors, which are techniques that draw comparisons. Others, such as alliteration, are lost in translation. Alliteration is the intentional repetition of the same initial sound of nearby words. Familiar examples include "*d*ead as a *d*oornail" and "*p*retty as a *p*icture." The biblical writers use alliteration many times, but they do so in Hebrew and Greek.

Most literary techniques in the Bible, however, are easily discerned if one knows what to look for. The comment in 2 Chronicles 1:15 that "the king made silver and gold as common in Jerusalem as stone" is a clear use of *hyperbole*, a deliberate exaggeration for rhetorical effect. Biblical writers frequently employ *merism*, a combining of opposite parts to signify a totality. The phrase "heaven and earth" (Ex. 31:17; Matt. 5:18), which signifies all of creation, is a well-known example. At times, biblical poetry is organized by an *acrostic*, a succession of lines that begin with consecutive letters of the alphabet. Psalm 119 is a huge acrostic. The first eight lines begin with the first letter of the Hebrew alphabet, the second series of eight begin with the second letter, and so on through the entirety of the Hebrew alphabet. Psalm 119 wasn't downloaded into the head of the writer; it took deliberate planning and creativity.

Two of the most common literary techniques are associated with prophetic messaging. Both Old and New Testament writers use symbols known broadly in the ancient world. The book of Daniel describes four beasts coming up out of the sea (Dan. 7:1–8). The beasts symbolize earthly empires. This technique is known from other ancient books outside the Bible that describe events related to an apocalypse. Biblical writers also employed typology. A *type* is basically a nonverbal prophecy—a person, event, or institution that foreshadows something to come. The classic example is the Passover lamb, which Paul tells us conceptually represented Christ (1 Cor. 5:7). Paul also sees Adam as a type, or foreshadowing, of Jesus (Rom. 5).

I don't have the space to discuss all the literary devices used by biblical writers. It's no exaggeration to say that every chapter in the Bible employs at least one. To better understand Scripture, we need to be alert to the strategies of communication the biblical writers employ. The more alert we are, the better we can follow their thinking.

CHAPTER 20

The Biblical Writers Didn't Always Intend to Be Taken Literally

I play a lot of fantasy baseball and football. I usually do okay and have even won some leagues. But occasionally I have a team that's just horrible. Whether it's due to injuries, happenstance, or my own poor decisions, some of my teams have stunk.

You all know that when I say my team "stank," I don't mean that literally. There's no awful aroma that wafts out of my computer screen when I'm looking at my lowly place in the league standings. But my estimation of my team—as evidenced by its performance—is nevertheless *real*.

This example illustrates a fallacy that is commonly embedded in the minds of Bible interpreters—we must interpret the Bible literally if we take its contents to be real. Put in reverse, the flawed assumption is that someone must be denying what the Bible says is real if they understand something in the Bible in a way other than "literalness." That simply isn't true.

Nonliteral interpretation does *not* mean "not real." We know this from everyday experience. My fantasy team is just one illustration. We can describe an exceptionally large man as a "mountain" or an unethical person as a "snake" or "rat." We know intuitively, because of our worldview experience, that these descriptions should not be taken literally. Nevertheless, their metaphorical meaning can be entirely accurate and true.

The same thing goes on in Scripture, but because we aren't thinking like an ancient person, we make the mistake of literalizing what was never intended to be understood that way. For example, the Old Testament refers to "Leviathan" in passages like Psalm 74:14 and Isaiah 27:1. These passages and others do not refer to literal prehistoric beasts or sea monsters. We know from literature outside the Bible that Leviathan was a metaphor or symbol for the wildness of the sea or chaotic disorder that threatened human existence. When the biblical writers have God taming Leviathan, it's a metaphorical—and true—statement that God has power over creation.

Biblical writers use a range of symbols and expressions that they never intended their audience to consider literally. These instances inform us very clearly that inspiration includes a lot of content that doesn't require or intend literal interpretation. Just because words show up in the Bible doesn't mean that their usage is different than in any other human writing or discourse. Inspiration doesn't bring literalism with it. We need to keep this in mind consistently in order to understand Scripture. If we don't, we force a flawed idea of our own onto the biblical text.

CHAPTER 21

The Biblical Writers Used Translations of the Bible

When I was teaching full-time, I'd occasionally hear students lament having to read the Bible in translation. Some would even wonder if they could trust their translations. I would tell students they need not worry about the issue since biblical writers used them.

I'm speaking primarily about how the New Testament writers quote the Old Testament. The New Testament was written in Greek. The Old Testament was written primarily in Hebrew, with a few portions written in Aramaic. When New Testament writers quote the Old Testament, they usually use something called the Septuagint, which was an ancient Greek translation of the Hebrew Old Testament.

It's interesting to note that the Septuagint wasn't always literal in its translation of the Old Testament. That didn't bother the New Testament writers. For example, a pretty literal rendering of Amos 9:11–12 reads like this:

In that day I will raise up the booth of David that is fallen, and repair its breaches, and raise up its ruins, and rebuild it as in the days of old, that they may possess the remnant of Edom and all the nations who are called by my name.

In literal terms, the prophecy seems to be about repairing a physical structure, perhaps a tent booth (Deut. 16:13–16) or a wall. Many readers would anticipate the prophecy is about the rebuilding of David's house or, by extension, his dynasty. The result would be the "remnant of Edom and all the nations" would be possessed by "David's booth."

Luke quotes this passage in Acts 15:16–17 and the wording changes: "I will rebuild the tent of David that has fallen; . . . that the remnant of mankind may seek the Lord, and all the gentiles who are called by my name."

Notice that Edom becomes "mankind" in Luke's rendering, while "nations" becomes the more specific "gentiles." The reason for the difference is that Luke is using the Septuagint. Edomites in the Old Testament were estranged relatives to Israel. In the context of Acts 15, because of Jesus, David's heir, the gentiles and *everyone* estranged from God can now be part of the people of God. The Septuagint translation actually makes the theological point of Amos 9 more clear, despite its "more than literal" wording.

The lesson is twofold: (1) the biblical writers were not afraid to use translations, so we shouldn't be afraid either; and (2) sometimes literalism isn't the best way to read something.

PART 4

LET THE FIRST FIVE BOOKS OF THE BIBLE BE WHAT THEY ARE

CHAPTER 22

The Creation Stories Target the Beliefs of Other Ancient Religions

Even people who've never read the Bible know that it talks about the creation of the world. They've heard, "In the beginning, God created the heavens and the earth" (Gen. 1:1). Because of our current cultural climate, though, the verse—and even the idea—is controversial to say the least. Our culture is a product of the seventeenth-century Enlightenment and the progress of science since then, particularly with respect to the rise of Darwin's theory of evolution. *None* of that was in the mind of the biblical writers.

The creation stories in the Bible don't aim to articulate modern scientific theories. By definition they couldn't, since they come from a premodern era. God wasn't dispensing advanced knowledge either, since no one who received the Bible prior to the modern period would have understood it. The whole enterprise of inspiration was aimed at bringing people truths they *could* understand, not transmitting cryptic knowledge to an intellectual elite.

The creation stories were designed to teach crucial theological ideas. They were deliberately written in ways that take shots at foreign gods and their (alleged) creative powers. But the effort is largely lost on us since most of what's going on in the text can only be discerned by people who read Hebrew and, just as importantly, people who shared the same worldview of the writers.

What's happening in Genesis 1 would have been obvious to anyone familiar with the competing creation stories from ancient Egypt, Babylon, and Canaan. For example, Genesis 1:1–3, which identifies God as the creator, follows the grammar, syntax, and themes of the Babylonian tale known as *Enuma Elish*, in which Marduk orders creation. The reference to "the deep" draws on Canaanite beliefs about the ordering of the world from the primeval waters. The same is true for creation passages outside Genesis. Psalm 74:12–17 links creation to God's slaying of a great sea beast. Ancient readers would have known that was a backhanded slap in the face to Baal, who defeats the sea dragon in Canaanite myths. The notion that God created by the spoken word (Gen. 1:3) is a direct attack on Egyptian creation beliefs preserved in *The Memphite Theology*, where the god Ptah was thought to speak everything into existence.

The biblical authors were clever and fearless in putting forth their fundamental theological claim: *the world of human experience is the product of the creative power of the God of Israel and no other god, period*. We process Genesis in light of our own age and intellectual battles. To do that is to impose a foreign context on the Bible. When critics chide the Bible for not being scientific, it is they who are ignorant. It is intellectually bankrupt to criticize something for not being what it was never intended to be. The claim of the biblical writers was a supernatural one, affirming the reality of a creator. We need that message even more today than ever, since our worldview is predisposed to rejecting the idea of God.

CHAPTER 23

Old Testament Genealogies Were Not Intended to Be Precise Indicators of the Age of the Earth

The genealogies of Genesis 5 are significant for understanding the Old Testament, but not in the way they are often referenced.

Since the seventeenth century, Bible readers have presumed that the genealogies of the Old Testament were written to provide a chronology for the history of the world. That notion was popularized in 1650 with the publication of Bishop James Ussher's *Annales veteris testamenti, a prima mundi origine deducti* ("Annals of the Old Testament, deduced from the first origins of the world"). Ussher's chronology used the genealogies to date the creation of the world to October 23, 4004 BC.

There are many problems with Ussher's chronology. It would, for example, put the flood at the time of the building of the Great Pyramid at Giza. Even if the flood was a regional and not a global event, it would have made the construction of this pyramid unworkable due to its proximity to the Nile and the Nile Delta. Egyptian records prior to and after the Great Pyramid's construction say nothing about a great flood during this time.

However, the real problems with Ussher's work are biblical. Ussher was unaware of certain things that are common knowledge in biblical scholarship today. For example, manuscripts of the

Hebrew Bible do not all agree when it comes to the genealogical sequence or year numbers of the preflood individuals listed in Genesis 5. The sequence of the generations in Genesis 4 and 5 is also not identical. This has led scholars over the years to propose that the genealogies are selective, which is obvious from the genealogies of Jesus in the New Testament.

While gaps are possible, there are other issues that speak to a deliberate construction to the genealogies. Several scholars have proposed that the year numbers in Genesis 5 have a mathematical explanation—in effect, a cypher or code—meant to telegraph information about the individuals in the list. However, none of the proposals has won a consensus of acceptance. Another approach has observed that genealogies from contemporary literature follow a pattern evident in Genesis 5. Specifically, several genealogies from the Old Babylonian period arrange names by tens even when the results do not account for people known from other sources to have lived in the same periods. In Genesis 5 there are ten generations before the flood, and ten after the flood. The listing may therefore be selective.

In any event, though the precise reason for the genealogical structure may not be conclusively understood, we must avoid interpreting them outside their ancient context. Forcing them into a service for which they were not intended isn't good interpretation.

CHAPTER 24

The Covenant Sign of Circumcision Was a Theological Statement for Israelite Men *and Women*

The story of Abraham and Sarah is at the core of the story of Israel. God called Abraham (Gen. 12:1–3; 15:1–6) and told him that he would make his offspring like the sand of the sea and the stars of the sky. There was just one problem. Abraham and his wife were old.

Sarah, in fact, was well past child-bearing age and did not conceive a child for several years after God's initial promise (Gen. 16:1–6; Heb. 11:11). Her inability to conceive led to Sarah's proposal that Abraham have children with her handmaid, Hagar. The result was the birth of Ishmael, whom God told Abraham in no uncertain terms was *not* the fulfillment of his original promise (Gen. 17:15–21; Heb. 11:17–18). God would enable Sarah to have a child.

God of course kept his promise. Abraham and Sarah had Isaac. God stepped in and made it clear to both Abraham and Sarah that Ishmael was not the fulfillment of his promise. Sarah was the mother God intended for the promised child. To commemorate that miracle, God gave them *both* a recurring sign of his covenant faithfulness: circumcision (Gen. 17:1–14).

The sign of the covenant meant that every male in Abraham's

household had to be circumcised. The requirement extended to all males born to every family in the nation of Israel because all Israelites were descendants of Abraham through Isaac.

Circumcision seems like an odd sign, not only because of the physical nature of the mark, but also because it seems so one-sided. Of what possible relevance could circumcision have for Israelite women? What's the point in the first place?

Because of the sexual nature of the sign of circumcision, the ritual mark was an important theological reminder to both genders. The sign would have taken the mind of both men and women back to the fact that they and their children only existed because of divine intervention.

Women would also be reminded of the importance of having husbands who were members of the Israelite community to pass on the bloodline of Abraham, Isaac, and Jacob. Bearing children to gentile men in Old Testament times would have been a covenant transgression unless the man joined the people of Israel (which required circumcision).

As unusual as the sign of circumcision seems to us today, it was a theological statement in its time. This is one important role of ritual—to transport and then fix the mind to a transcendent idea.

CHAPTER 25

The Rebellion at the Tower of Babel Frames the Rest of Biblical History

I mentioned the Tower of Babel story (Gen. 11:1–9) in chapter 11, which examined how ancient biblical people understood their world. Genesis 11 isn't the only passage that talks about that event. Deuteronomy 32:8–9, one of the most important passages in the Old Testament for understanding the worldview of the people of the Bible, does as well. The ESV translates it this way:

> When the Most High gave to the nations their inheritance,
>> when he divided humankind,
> he fixed the borders of the peoples
>> according to the number of the sons of God.
> But the LORD's portion is his people,
>> Jacob his allotted heritage.

When God divided the nations—the punishment at Babel when the languages were confused—he distributed them among "the sons of God." Some Bible translations have "sons of Israel" instead of "sons of God." But *Israel didn't exist at the time of the Tower of Babel*. God called Abraham and began the nation of Israel after *Babel* (Gen. 12). "Sons of Israel" can't be right. "Sons of God" is also what the Dead Sea Scrolls say, the oldest manuscripts of the Bible. The ESV has it right.

Deuteronomy 4:19–20 is the opposite side of that coin. That passage has God allotting these other gods to the nations he dispersed at Babel. These two passages associated with the rebellion at Babel are the Old Testament's explanation of why the other nations worship other gods: it's divine punishment from the God of Israel.

So the Tower of Babel event is similar to Romans 1, where Paul tells us that God gave humankind over to its own rebellion. Because the nations would not obey him, God basically gave humanity over to lesser gods. God gave them what they wanted—other gods to follow. The result was self-destruction and idolatry.

This event, alongside the call of Abraham and origin of Israel that followed (Gen. 12), frames the rest of the Old Testament. It explains the spiritual conflict of Israel's God against other gods and the nations in hostile opposition to Israel. Sadly, the gods of the other nations seduced God's own portion, Israel (Deut. 17:1–3; 29:22–28; 32:17).

This conflict extends into the New Testament as well. Paul rarely uses the word "demons" to describe the spiritual opposition we face. He uses words like "principalities," "powers," "thrones," "dominions," and "authorities," which all convey the idea of geographical rulership. The message is that the whole world is under the dominion of unseen powers of darkness, save for those who are in Christ. Babel explains why that is so.

CHAPTER 26

Neither God nor the Israelites Looked at Old Testament Laws as Equal in Character and Importance

James 2:10 says, "For whoever keeps the whole law but fails in one point has become accountable for all of it" (NRSV). On one level, the meaning is clear: break one of God's laws and you become a lawbreaker. The meaning of "accountable for all of it" is less clear, since we are accountable to God's law whether we break it or not. The idea actually being communicated is that guilt before God is the result of breaking any law, from the most innocuous to the most heinous. Guilt is guilt.

But does that mean that God considers every violation to be the same level of wickedness? Every sinner is guilty, but are all sins equally awful? The answer is no.

The Bible is quite clear on this matter. First, just as in our own legal/judicial system, Old Testament laws could be divided into categories. One example would be case law—laws that depend on certain conditions. These Old Testament laws are expressed by if-then statements ("If X happens, then Y is the punishment"). These laws are hypothetical: the nature of the crime (and therefore its punishment) can change with a situation. Other laws are strict prohibitions, regardless of the situation. They aren't hypothetical. These are usually expressed with the familiar "thou shalt not" phrase.

Second, Old Testament laws did not carry the same punishments. While any violation made one guilty before God, the fact that God's law did not demand equal punishment for *any* violation demonstrates that all violations were *not* viewed the same way. The notion that God is "just as angry" with the person who steals an ox as he is with a blasphemer might make for good preaching, but one was punished by remuneration (Ex. 22:1) and the other by death (Lev. 24:16). The outcome was far from the same. And in the Old Testament, death penalty offenses could not be atoned for by sacrifice.

Third, of the many laws in the Torah, God himself singled out one that was fundamentally important to him, and therefore to his covenantal promises with his children, Israel. Loving God—being loyal to him above all gods—was fundamental to possessing the promised land (e.g., Lev. 26; Deut. 4:25–27, 39–40). Loving loyalty to God was the greatest commandment (Mark 12:30–31).

The lesson is not that we can take solace in not being as bad as the next person. We are all guilty before God and undeserving of eternal life (Rom. 6:23). We all need the same grace. Instead, the lesson is that God is not unbalanced and cruel, viewing all acts of sin and evil the same way. His laws are not capricious.

CHAPTER 27

The Biblical Concept of Holiness Includes, but Is Not Limited To, Moral Behavior

Holiness is one of the more frequent characterizations of God in the Bible. Unfortunately, what the concept actually means is frequently misunderstood. In our modern context, holiness is typically associated with moral behavior, particularly in a negative sense—avoiding certain behaviors produces or demonstrates holiness. The behaviors to be avoided are either the moral prohibitions in the Bible or the activities a Christian subculture does not associate with God's own character.

Holiness in the Bible relates to personal conduct, but the concept is much broader. The description "holy" is applied to an amazingly diverse list of things, including: God (Lev. 11:44–45); people (Lev. 21:7), days (Gen. 2:3), ground (Ex. 3:5), offerings (Lev. 2:3); garments (Ex. 28:2), oil (Ex. 30:25), events (Ex. 12:16; Lev. 23:27), structures (Ex. 26:33; Ps. 5:7), water (Num. 5:17), divine beings (Deut. 33:2), utensils (1 Kings 8:4), and bread (Ex. 29:34). Since many of these items are inanimate objects, moral purity is not in the picture.

In simplest terms, one thing unites the items on this list: they are all *associated with* God. Holiness is therefore linked to the person and presence of God. For that reason, scholars have concluded that the best way to understand holiness is God's utter uniqueness—his "otherness" in relation to all things. When a person, place, or thing is called holy, the point is that the person, place, or thing is set aside exclusively for God's use, service, or remembrance. Whatever is holy is by definition not to be used by, attributed to, or associated with any other person, place, or thing. Holiness speaks of uniqueness because God is unique.

For this reason, the antonym of holiness is not a word like "evil" or "wickedness." Rather, terms like "common" or "ordinary" better describe the polar opposite of holiness. If something was for everyday use in Israel, it was not holy. That which was holy was exclusively devoted to God and his service and worship. There was no middle ground.

Behavior becomes part of a discussion of holiness in its relationship to other concepts, such as clean and unclean or purity and impurity, terms that spoke of one's ritual fitness for being in God's presence (which was considered "sacred space") or participating in religious rituals and practices.

The list above demonstrates that holiness encompassed every area of Israelite life. The effect was practical. Israelites were regularly reminded of God—his absolute otherness and moral perfection. But because they had the Law and were in covenant relationship to that same God, Israelites were also regularly reminded that this transcendent being loved them and chose them from among all people.

CHAPTER 28

Some of the Strangest Ideas in Biblical Law Teach Important Points of Biblical Theology

Certain laws in the Old Testament make little sense to modern readers. For example, in Leviticus we read:

> If a woman conceives and bears a male child, then she shall be unclean seven days. As at the time of her menstruation, she shall be unclean. . . . She shall not touch anything holy, nor come into the sanctuary, until the days of her purifying are completed. (Lev. 12:1–7)

> When any man has a discharge from his body, his discharge is unclean. And this is the law of his uncleanness for a discharge: whether his body runs with his discharge, or his body is blocked up by his discharge, it is his uncleanness. (Lev. 15:2–3)

> If a man has an emission of semen, he shall bathe his whole body in water and be unclean until the evening. (Lev. 15:16)

> When a woman has a discharge, and the discharge in her body is blood, she shall be in her menstrual impurity for

seven days, and whoever touches her shall be unclean until
the evening. (Lev. 15:19)

Why are these discharges, all of which are clearly natural,
considered unclean in biblical law? In part, these help everyone
remember that uncleanness was not a moral issue. Rather, uncleanness was concerned with whether a person was fit to enter sacred
space—territory occupied by God's presence or which had been
set aside for God.

We associate being excluded from entering the divine presence
with sin, but these discharges are clearly not sin. Scripture never
describes them that way. Instead, the unclean status taught the
Israelites, and can teach us, important theological truths.

Blood and semen had something in common in the Israelite
worldview: they were life fluids. Leviticus 17:11 says, "The life of
the flesh is in the blood." Israelites knew that severe loss of blood
meant death. Semen, of course, was where human life came from.
Although the Israelites were scientifically and medically primitive
by today's standards, they knew where babies came from.

Blood and semen meant life. Their loss was therefore symbolic
of the loss of life. Consequently, forbidding a person who had lost
"life force" was a way of reinforcing a simple theological point: God
gives life, and his presence means life, not death.

Other biblical laws derive from this rationale. Israelite law held
human life as sacred because humans were God's imagers. Our
perspective should be the same.

CHAPTER 29

Biblical Writers Took the Concept of Holy Ground Seriously

To the ancient Israelite, the world was a perilous place. Not only did most people live a subsistence lifestyle, where daily bread was a literal concern, but they were surrounded by hostile supernatural forces. God's choice of Israel was a blessing, but it came on the heels of the terrible judgment at the Tower of Babel, where all the other nations were allotted to the dominion of lesser gods (Deut. 32:8–9). Israel was alone against the world.

This worldview operated in tandem with an idea fundamental to biblical theology: the holiness of God. God was holy; therefore, the things associated with him were holy or had to be made holy. Wherever the presence of God was to be found, that place was by definition holy ground. The most obvious example is the territory encompassed by the tabernacle and, later, the temple. Only priests— people who had been made holy (set apart or "sanctified" by ritual acts) were allowed on that holy ground.

The concept was actually broader. While the Israelites journeyed to the promised land, holy ground was also equated with the entire camp of Israel since the ark located within the Holy of Holies was at the center of the camp (Num. 2–3). This is why, in the Day of Atonement ceremony, the goat that bore the sins of the nation was driven out of the camp (Lev. 16). Sin has no place on holy ground.

Once the Israelites settled in the promised land—God's domain—the entire land was considered holy ground. Everywhere outside Israel was unholy.

Some odd episodes in the Old Testament are understandable in light of this worldview. In 2 Kings 5 we read the story of Naaman, the Syrian captain who had leprosy. Once miraculously healed, Naaman asked the prophet Elisha if he could load his mule with dirt to take home with him. The request seems ridiculous, but isn't. Naaman recognized that Yahweh of Israel was the true God (2 Kings 5:15), so Naaman wanted to take some holy ground back with him to Syria, which was ruled by another god, Rimmon (2 Kings 5:18). Similarly, when David was driven out of Israelite territory, he complains that he had been told to go worship other gods (1 Sam. 26:17–20). We might wonder why David would care. Didn't he realize he could worship God everywhere? He actually didn't. The tabernacle and the priesthood were in Israel—holy ground. He was not.

This conceptual framework is significant for New Testament theology. The presence of God no longer lives in the temple or any one place. Instead, the Presence dwells in each believer (Eph. 2:22; 3:17; James 4:5). We are the temple of God, individually and corporately (1 Cor. 3:16; 6:19). We are holy ground, and we ought to take the concept as seriously as biblical people did.

CHAPTER 30

Old Testament Sacrifices Weren't Primarily about Individual Forgiveness for Sin

The sacrificial system of the Old Testament isn't easy to understand. Not only is the system convoluted and complex, but statements about its purpose seem to contradict each other. On one hand, Hebrews 10:4 asserts, "It is impossible for the blood of bulls and goats to take away sins." On the other hand, one of the results of various sacrifices in the book of Leviticus is that the person (or nation) will "be forgiven" (e.g., Lev. 4:20, 26; 5:10).

The problem of this apparent inconsistency is a matter of both terminology and taking a more careful look at Old Testament sacrifices. There are indeed certain passages where sacrifices do indeed result in "being forgiven," but exactly what that means requires explanation. Most of the time, however, blood sacrifice has nothing to do with addressing individual sin.

The burnt, grain, and peace offerings (Lev. 1–3) were basically gifts to God. They were positive responses to the fellowship relationship between the one bringing the offering and the Lord. They were offered to enhance the well-being of that relationship, not to earn salvation. The so-called "sin offering" (Lev. 4–5) and "guilt offering" (Lev. 5–7) are less comprehensible to us. Part of the problem is that the translated English names of these offerings are misleading. They are better understood as "the purification offering" and "the reparation offering." The blood of these offerings was *never* applied to the one bringing the offering, so there is no sense that the worshipper was being cleansed of sin. The blood was only used to purify the sanctuary and its furniture. These offerings were designed to purge the sanctuary and its accoutrements from ritual defilement to maintain the sanctity of sacred space.

It is crucial to grasp the *biblical* meaning of Hebrew terms translated "atone" (*kipper*) and "forgive" (*salach*). Contrary to popular teaching, the first term does *not* mean "to cover." Rather, *kipper* means "to purge" or "wipe clean" with respect to defilement of the sanctuary. This makes sense given the use of the blood in the offerings noted above. The second term is best translated "become clean" or "be purified." This again makes sense since the blood was applied to the sanctuary. This helps us understand passages that speak of a person being forgiven. These blood sacrifices purged and purified the sanctuary from defilement that could be brought to it by people who either committed a moral offense (i.e., sinned) or who "inadvertently" (as opposed to defiantly) became unclean and were no longer holy (Lev. 4:2, 22; 5:15). People were "forgiven" in the sense that they would no longer bring contamination into sacred space. There was no sacrifice at all in the Old Testament for defiant sin (e.g., Num. 15:30–31).

The blood sacrifices therefore meant that the one making the offering no longer threatened sacred space. While the contaminating effect of inadvertent sin was dealt with, sacrifices didn't offer the same permanent forgiveness and removal of sin as Jesus does.

CHAPTER 31

Deuteronomy Is One Long Sermon by Moses to the Israelites

Like Leviticus and Numbers, Deuteronomy can be confusing since it seems like nothing is happening in Israel's journey. It often seems like just a lot of talking. That's because that's what it is. Deuteronomy presents its content as a lengthy speech or sermon by Moses just before the Israelites try for the second time to enter the promised land. Deuteronomy therefore begins with the end of the forty-year wandering in the desert—a punishment imposed by God for their failure to enter the land in faith for fear of the giant Anakim in Numbers 13.

It's because of this unfortunate history that the sermon of Moses starts out by rehearsing Israel's history, warts and all, from its miraculous beginning with Abraham and Sarah to its miserable failure at Kadesh-barnea (Deut. 1). Once Israel gets that painful reminder, Deuteronomy repeats the laws given at Sinai, but with some changes that reflect life *in* the land (Deut. 5–26). This is why this book is referred to in English Bibles as "Deuteronomy"—a title made up of two words that mean "second law" (*deuteros* + *nomos*).

The effect of all this is that the words of Moses are taking the people spiritually and emotionally back to Sinai so they can start over again.

But Deuteronomy is far more than a repetition of a long list of laws. Part of Moses's sermon is designed to elicit a public response from the people that *this time—and for good*—they will obey God in faith. Accordingly, chapters 27–30 are framed as a public covenant commitment ceremony to solidify that decision. It's serious content too, since two whole chapters (28–30) comprise a long list of curses that will happen to the people if they forsake the Lord as their God. Specifically, the promise of the land itself is tied to obedience to God:

> But if you will not obey the voice of the LORD your God or be careful to do all his commandments and his statutes that I command you today, then all these curses shall come upon you and overtake you. . . . The LORD will send on you curses, confusion, and frustration in all that you undertake to do, until you are destroyed and perish quickly on account of the evil of your deeds, because you have forsaken me. The LORD will make the pestilence stick to you until he has consumed you off the land that you are entering to take possession of it. . . . The LORD will bring you and your king whom you set over you to a nation that neither you nor your fathers have known. And there you shall serve other gods of wood and stone. And you shall become a horror, a proverb, and a byword among all the peoples where the LORD will lead you away. (Deut. 28:15–21, 36–37)

Sadly, these last statements reflect what eventually came to pass when Israel was exiled from the land. Deuteronomy is a powerful book. We need to heed it more carefully than Israel did.

CHAPTER 32

Ancient Israelites Believed the Gods of the Nations Were Real

I've brought up Deuteronomy 32 a couple of times already. Part of that important Old Testament chapter refers back to the Tower of Babel incident where the earth was divided into the nations listed in Genesis 10. Deuteronomy 32:8 (cf. Deut. 4:19–20) tells us that God allotted the nations among the sons of God when he decided to punish the rebellion at Babel and divide the earth. Israel would thereafter be the Lord's portion on earth (Deut. 32:9). Deuteronomy 4:19–20, a parallel passage, tells us these sons of God were the "host of heaven," a term also used in 1 Kings 22:19. In 1 Kings, the host of heaven are the spiritual beings assembled before God who help decide wicked King Ahab's fate.

We also saw earlier how this incident, as described in Deuteronomy 32:8–9, led to a cosmic-geographical worldview, where Israel was holy ground and all the other nations were under the dominion of hostile gods. The story of the Old Testament is basically Israel and its God against the nations and their gods. For ancient Israelites, these sons of God who presided over other nations were real entities. Spiritual warfare was the Israelites' daily reality.

Another verse in Deuteronomy 32 drives home this point. Just after discussing how God divided up the nations and allotted them to lesser gods, Deuteronomy 32:15–17 has this sad refrain:

And Jeshurun grew fat, and he kicked;

you grew fat, you bloated, and you became obstinate;

and he abandoned God, his maker,

and he scoffed *at* the rock of his salvation.

They made him jealous with strange *gods*;

with detestable things they provoked him.

They sacrificed to the demons, not God,

to gods whom they had not known,

new *gods who* came from recent times;

their ancestors had not known them. (LEB)

Verse 17 tells us that, despite repeated warnings (Deut. 17:1–3; 29:24–26), Israel turned to idolatry—Israelites worshipped the gods of other nations. Notice that these entities are referred to as *demons*. The gods of the other nations are not mere idols; they are real spiritual entities hostile to God and his people.

Interestingly, Paul quotes Deuteronomy 32:17 in his discussion of eating food offered to idols in 1 Corinthians 10:19–22. But Paul doesn't use only the word *idols* in his warning. He explains that there are spiritual entities behind and beyond idols—demons (1 Cor. 10:20–22). Biblical people believed in unseen spiritual conflict. It was real to them. Is it real to you?

CHAPTER 33

God Was Present in Human Form in the Old Testament

The time of Jesus wasn't the first time in the Bible that God appeared on earth as a man. There are several places in the Old Testament where God comes in human form—even to the point of embodiment. In fact, these appearances became reference points for New Testament writers to talk about Jesus.

For example, in several passages, the "word of the Lord" appears to prophetic figures like Abraham (Gen. 15:1, 4), Samuel (1 Sam. 3:1, 7, 21), and Jeremiah (Jer. 1:2, 4, 11). In these instances, the "word of the Lord" was *visible*. In other words, the reference is not just to a voice inside the head. In Jeremiah's case, the "word of the Lord"—identified as God himself in the passage—*reaches out his hand and touches* the prophet (Jer. 1:9). These passages and others like them are where the apostle John gets his idea that Jesus was "the word" who was God—the word made flesh (John 1:1–3, 14).

Further evidence for God in human form in the Old Testament is the Angel of the Lord. In Exodus 23:20–21 God tells Moses:

> Behold, I send an angel before you to guard you on the way and to bring you to the place that I have prepared. Pay careful attention to him and obey his voice; do not rebel against him, for he will not pardon your transgression, *for my name is in him.*

The word translated "angel" in the Old Testament means "messenger," and so the "angel of the Lord" is a divine being sent to do a particular task. The key thing to notice in Exodus 23 is that this particular angel has the "name" of God in him. Other passages make it clear that this is another way to refer to God himself. For example, the angel with God's name in him was assigned by God to lead the Israelites to the promised land. Judges 2:1–3 tells us that the angel accomplishes that task. But in Deuteronomy 4:37–38 we read that God took Israel out of Egypt and defeated her enemies to conquer the land through God's "presence." In other words, God's presence was in the angel. Interestingly enough, in the New Testament, Jude 5 shows Jesus delivering the Israelites from Egypt and defeating their enemies!

Genesis 48:15–16 makes this explicit. When Jacob blessed Joseph's children, he prayed:

> The *God* before whom my fathers, Abraham and Isaac, walked,
> > The *God* who has shepherded me all my life unto this day
> *The angel* who has redeemed me from all evil
> > may *he* bless the boys. (LEB)

The text doesn't read, "may *they* bless the boys" but "may *he* bless the boys." The wording treats God and the angel as one.

There are other passages that show God in human form before Jesus. God wasn't born of a woman in these passages, but they prepared people for that event.

PART 5

LET THE HISTORICAL BOOKS BE WHAT THEY ARE

CHAPTER 34

Archaeology Can Validate but Not Prove the Bible

Many Bible students are fascinated by archaeology. There's a certain mystique about recovering something hidden from human eyes for thousands of years. Archaeological discoveries can tell us a lot about the past. Artifacts can tell us something about how people lived. Texts can tell us what they thought or saw. Because archaeology provides these windows into the past, it's important for understanding the Bible.

Unfortunately, what archaeology can do for the Bible is often overstated. Popular apologetics books talk a lot about how archaeology "proves" the Bible, but that's misleading. While it's true that the names of biblical characters have been found on tablets and inscriptions, archaeology has never produced a text or artifact that precisely points to any biblical character before the time of David. For example, finding "Jacob" inscribed somewhere isn't necessarily a reference to the biblical character. A lot of people at the time could have borne that name.

Does that mean that there is no archaeological evidence for Bible characters like Abraham, Isaac, Jacob, Joseph, Moses, Joshua, Gideon, Samson, and Samuel? Yes. But the issue needs to be framed differently. If we ask, "Does that mean that there is no archaeological evidence for the events, historical circumstances, lifestyle portrayals, and religious beliefs of those biblical characters?" the answer would be the polar opposite. Archaeology has produced a lot of evidence that demonstrates the details of biblical stories are quite plausible (e.g., marriage customs and treaty structures). It has also produced artifacts that show a biblical detail about history was correct even though correlating proof was lacking for many years (e.g., Belshazzar's rule over Babylon). These achievements are important for defending biblical validity.

Something archaeology can never do, though, is prove the theological statements of the Bible. You can't dig up God. And even if archaeologists find the walls of the biblical Jericho toppled down and burned (and some would say they have), Jericho's ruins cannot prove that *God* knocked them down. That's a theological assertion. Since God's existence and power is beyond the realm of science, they are also beyond the realm of archaeology. The coherence of the Bible's truth claims needs to be defended on other grounds, such as sound logic.

Archaeology is a valuable tool for validating the circumstances of biblical events. It is dangerous, however, to exaggerate its contribution. Claims that overstate evidence are bound to be overturned. Theological truths should not be put in jeopardy by careless apologetics.

CHAPTER 35

"Israel" Doesn't Always Mean "Israel" in the Old Testament

Most Bible students will know that Israel's first three kings were Saul, David, and Solomon. They were the only three kings to rule over all twelve tribes, what scholars call the *united monarchy*. The complete kingdom was known in the Old Testament as Israel, since the twelve tribes of Israel swore allegiance to the same king. Solomon's reign ends in 1 Kings 11. That means the united monarchy—the lives of Saul, David, and Solomon—are covered in 1–2 Samuel and 1 Kings 1–10.

After Solomon died, ten of the tribes seceded from the nation and formed their own kingdom. From that point on, the way biblical writers referred to both political entities can be confusing.

The two tribes left after the secession were Judah and Benjamin. The latter was a tiny tribe and geographical area. Judah was much larger and the place where Jerusalem, the former capital of the united monarchy, was located. Judah was the tribe of David, whom God had chosen and whose lineage God had declared by a covenant was the only legitimate dynasty for rule over his people (2 Sam. 7). Both Judah and Benjamin were located in the southern section of the promised land. As a result, the southern kingdom of these two tribes became known as Judah.

The ten tribes who had defected from David's dynasty were a

different story. Since they comprised the bulk of the land and the tribes, they retained the name "Israel" as a political entity. That means that, after the kingdom split in 1 Kings 11, "Israel" often refers only to the ten tribes. Most of the territory covered by these ten tribes covered the northern part of the promised land, and so this "Israel" is also referred to as the northern kingdom.

To make things more complicated, the ten-tribe nation of "Israel" also went by other names. The central hill country of the land was dominated by the territory of the tribe of Ephraim. Jereboam, the first king of the renegade ten tribes, built his capital (Shechem) in Ephraim. However, Ephraim's own capital had been Samaria. After the time of Jereboam, Samaria became the capital of the northern kingdom. Consequently, the ten-tribe northern kingdom of "Israel" was also known as Ephraim and Samaria.

All of this has an impact on our reading of the Old Testament's historical material after 1 Kings 11, as well as books of the prophets who lived after the original kingdom split. "Israel" in those books mostly refers to only ten tribes and is interchangeable with Ephraim and Samaria.

CHAPTER 36

Chronicles Contains Propaganda by Design

I n English Bibles, the books of 1–2 Chronicles are grouped with the historical books: Joshua, Judges, Ruth, 1–2 Samuel, and 1–2 Kings. The reason is that the content of 1–2 Chronicles overlaps with the books of Samuel and Kings. The books of 1–2 Chronicles present the story of the Israelite monarchy, both in the days when it was united over all twelve tribes and afterward when it was divided into two kingdoms.

While the books of Chronicles follow the story of Israel's united monarchy under David and Solomon presented in Samuel and Kings, the accounts of their reigns in Chronicles are substantially different. The chronicler (the name given to whoever fashioned the history presented in 1–2 Chronicles) systematically censors the material of 1–2 Samuel.

Perhaps the best example of this censoring is the fact that David's lurid affair with Bathsheba and his subsequent arrangement of her husband Uriah's death (2 Samuel 11). The incident occurred in connection with David's military campaigns against Ammon and Syria (2 Sam. 10–11:1). While the chronicler details those campaigns, he says nothing about David's evil (1 Chron. 19–20). These omissions reflect a pattern whereby David and Solomon are portrayed only positively.

It's easy for us to read this as pure propaganda. In one sense, it is. But we must recall that the Old Testament in its final form does in fact include 1–2 Samuel and 1–2 Kings, so the Bible doesn't whitewash the sins of David and Solomon. Readers would not be deceived. Understanding what the chronicler does requires understanding his goal and context.

Scholars are unanimous that 1–2 Chronicles were written after the exile. In the Hebrew Bible's arrangement, these are the last two books. Both the northern and southern kingdoms had committed idolatry, worshipping other gods, flaunting God's law. The northern kingdom had forsaken David's dynasty, something God had also specifically instituted. These corporate rebellions had been the cause of God's wrath and the exile.

God's restoration of the kingdom of Judah after seventy years in exile was a second chance. The chronicler rewrote the nation's history with an eye toward reminding his readers of what had led to the debacle: forsaking David and his heir, Solomon, and worshipping other gods. The forgiven nation must be loyal to David's dynasty. There was no room for rebellion. The nation must honor God's chosen line as it worshipped God alone. Toward motivating that loyalty, the chronicler's account presents David and Solomon at their best—the glory days of the nation—to make people want that good life once more.

CHAPTER 37

Most of the Cities and Towns Mentioned in the Bible Have Not Been Excavated

If you asked someone where the events of the Bible took place, chances are you'd get an answer like "Israel" or "the Holy Land." That's of course true, but the statement is imprecise and, to a significant extent, quite incomplete.

There are hundreds of sites mentioned in the Bible that are connected to events in the biblical saga. Some are the setting for just one event, while others are crucial focus points for many episodes in the history of Israel or the work of Jesus and the apostles.

Only a small percentage of the places mentioned in the Bible have been excavated by archaeologists. Archaeology regularly yields information that illumines the biblical world and the stories we read in Scripture. The fact that many sites in Israel have not yet been excavated, or even discovered, is important for Bible students in several respects.

First, the circumstances of biblical events are often framed by their location. Biblical places often have a long history (positive or negative), and that history creates the backdrop for why a biblical writer may have included it in the story. By way of a more modern example, Robert E. Lee's refusal to accept President Lincoln's offer of command over the Army of the Potomac is comprehensible when we learn Lee was from Virginia. Lee was no apologist for slavery. Given the proximity of the army offered to him to his home state, Lee could not bear the thought of invading his home state and killing fellow Virginians. Lee's personal attachment to the geography of the situation prompted his decision. In terms of the Bible, when sites cannot be located or go unexcavated, some details of Bible interpretation remain unclear. Archaeology becomes a hermeneutical aid.

Second, excavation of sites often helps clear up a Bible difficulty or perceived error in the biblical text. The history of biblical scholarship has numerous examples of how archaeology clears up an apparent dilemma or lends credibility to biblical details. For example, an inscription discovered at the Tel Dan discovered in 1993 contains what most scholars regard as a verifiable reference to the "house of David." Seals (small pieces of pressed clay) bearing the names of biblical kings serve to validate their existence.

Archaeological work in Israel is a work in progress. When hostile critics attack the Bible on the flawed presumption that all the data that *could* illuminate the discussion has been discovered, their conclusion assumes too much.

CHAPTER 38

The Books of Joshua through 2 Kings Were Likely Written by the Same Person(s) at the Same Time

The first Old Testament book after the Torah, the book of Joshua, describes the conquest of the land of Canaan by the Israelites. Joshua marks the transition of the people of Israel to a settled nation. The books that follow it chronicle the nation's failure to drive out all the foreign inhabitants of the land, along with its consequences (Judges); the saga of one family during the period of the judges (Ruth); the end of the rule of local judges in favor of a monarchy of kings, particularly David (1–2 Samuel); and the sad story of how the monarchy fell into ruin after the end of the reign of Solomon, David's son (1–2 Kings). Collectively, those books take up a lot of space in the Old Testament, and a lot of the biblical story.

It may surprise you to learn that these books are anonymous. None of them name or even hint at an author. But they present a theologically unified picture of the cost of losing faith in God and living in disobedience to him. The books from Joshua to 2 Kings proclaim in one voice that the ultimate disastrous judgment of God on Israel (the exile) was due to the sins of the Israelites, especially the matter of idolatry. Each book builds the case in painstaking detail that the awful judgment of the exile was entirely justified. Anyone living during the dark days of the breakdown of the nation (or afterward) would only need to read Joshua through 2 Kings to know that Israel got what it deserved.

This chorus of warning and condemnation is the main reason why many scholars believe these books were written by the same person or persons and, therefore, at the same time. Because the condemnation of idolatry is so strong, and presented as fact in much of this material, scholars propose that the material was written sometime shortly after the northern kingdom of Israel (ten of the tribes) was taken into captivity by the Assyrians. How could this happen? Where was God? Joshua through 2 Kings answered those questions. God was there all the time, but Israel had turned her back on him. Consequently, God used the Assyrians to judge them.

At the same time, this terrible message was intended to save the remaining two tribes from the same fate. The people of Judah, the southern kingdom, could learn from the epic horror to stay loyal to God and his law, trusting him to protect them. Sadly, the southern kingdom faltered. God raised up prophets to direct the people back to himself, often by reminding them of what had happened to their relatives. But in the end, the last two tribes would suffer a similar end, this time at the hand of Babylon. But God anticipated the failure and vowed to keep a remnant of faithful believers alive—and send a future deliverer.

We need to read these books as the hindsight warnings they were. They provide us with valuable lessons about the human heart, the cost of sin, and God's mercy.

CHAPTER 39

Judges Weren't Kings

The book of Judges is largely an intentional contrast between the faithlessness of God's people and his own faithfulness. Repeatedly in Judges we read that Israel turned against God's laws and commands, suffered under foreign oppressors as a result, and then had to be bailed out of their misery by God. The first chapter sums it up: "And the people of Israel did what was evil in the sight of the LORD.... And they abandoned the LORD, the God of their fathers, who had brought them out of the land of Egypt. They went after other gods.... And they were in terrible distress. Then the LORD raised up judges, who saved them out of the hand of those who plundered them" (Judg. 2:11–12, 15–16).

When we see the word "judges," we think of people who decide legal cases and pass out sentences to criminals. That isn't who's in view here. Reading through the book of Judges makes it clear that, with the exception of Deborah (who actually did listen to complaints and make decisions for people; see Judg. 4:4–5), judges were military leaders that God raised up to defeat Israel's enemies.

The period of the judges was one of lawlessness. It was chaotic and unpredictable. Twice the book tells readers that "everyone did what was right in his own eyes" (Judg. 17:6; 21:25). On nearly ten occasions the author offers the blunt assessment that "Israel did what was evil in the sight of the LORD" (e.g., Judg. 2:11; 3:7).

Several analogies to the judges suggest themselves. The time of

103

the judges could be looked upon like the Wild West, when gangs of outlaws controlled towns and territories by fear, ignoring the law. That would make judges the equivalent of sheriffs or hired guns. Perhaps more familiar, we could think of Canaan at this time like the fictional Gotham. None of the judges had a cape and lived in the Batcave, but you get the idea. Judges were deliverers, the superheroes of their day.

Judges were not kings. They did not rule over all the tribes, or even any tribe. They did not have dynasties, although Gideon and his son Abimelech tried to pull that off (Judg. 6–9). Judges were a temporary solution to the problems of the time. They defeated foreign enemies and restored law and order, ushering in a time of peace until the next judge was needed (e.g., Judg. 3:11, 30). Their authority was regional. For example, sometimes Israel's oppressors only controlled specific cities (Judg. 3:12–14).

The book of Judges serves an important purpose. It offered a vivid argument for kingship as a permanent solution to foreign conquest. As we'll see, God had planned all along for Israel to have kings. Having a king wasn't a sin. But trusting a man instead of God was.

CHAPTER 40

God Intended All Along for Israel to Have a King

After the wars of Joshua and the conquering of the promised land, Israel fell into turmoil (Judg. 1). The conquest remained incomplete. Their failure was the result of apostasy—tolerating and even embracing other gods. As punishment, God allowed Israel to be overrun by foreign oppressors. The book of Judges chronicles that period, which was basically a repetitious cycle of apostasy, oppression, temporary repentance, and divinely appointed deliverance by a military leader referred to as a judge.

Samuel was a judge and served the people well. Unfortunately, his sons were corrupt and unreliable judges (1 Sam. 8:2–3). The Israelites saw an opportunity to demand something more permanent. They demanded Samuel appoint a king so they could be like the rest of the nations (1 Sam. 8:4–5). Samuel didn't like the idea and said so to both the Israelites and God (1 Sam. 8:6). God told him not to take it personally, since the request was really a rejection of God, not the prophet (1 Sam. 8:7–9).

The negative assessment has been taken by many Bible students as proof that kingship for Israel was evil. This is hard to reconcile with the fact that Deuteronomy 17:14–20 lays down rules for good kingship for Israel once it entered the land. Kingship is viewed positively even earlier than that. Genesis 49:10 says very plainly that the tribe of Judah would produce kings.

How do we reconcile the apparent conflict of interest? Clarity comes later in 1 Samuel 8. In verse five the people demanded, "Appoint for us a king to judge us like all the nations." The language changes a bit in verses 19–20: "There shall be a king over us, that we also may be like all the nations, and that our king may judge us and go out before us and fight our battles."

The desire for a king to go out and fight the nation's battles is the key to understanding why the request was offensive. In Israel's earlier history, it was God who had fought for Israel. God had defeated Egypt and her gods (Ex. 14–15), and he had brought Israel to the promised land in the form of an angel (Ex. 23:20–23). When Israel failed spiritually after Joshua died, the angel of the Lord forsook them, initiating the chaos of the period of the judges (Judg. 2:1–5).

Having a king wasn't the issue. Replacing God as military leader showed that Israel had not learned her lesson. There was no will to trust God with their security as Moses and Joshua had done. They wanted a tough guy. Their choice, Saul, looked the part (1 Sam. 9:1–2). God planned for Israel to have a king but one who had a heart that would trust in him. Eventually, they'd get one: David.

CHAPTER 41

The Book of Ruth Takes Place During the Days of the Judges

The period of the book of Judges was awful. The book runs through cycle after cycle of Israel's spiritual failure, God's punishment for their faithlessness by means of foreign oppressors, desperate cries for deliverance, and God sending a judge in response. Sin, suffer, despair, deliverance, repeat.

One of the key things to observe in the book is that the oppressors of God's people were foreigners—people to whom the land did not belong. At times God's instrument of punishment for sin was a people group whom Israel was supposed to have driven from the land but didn't. At other times, it was a people group from the outside. The point is this: the presence of foreigners meant bad things. They were unpopular.

This is the backdrop for the story of Ruth. The book opens with these statements:

> In the days when the judges ruled there was a famine in the land, and a man of Bethlehem in Judah went to sojourn in the country of Moab, he and his wife and his two sons. The name of the man was Elimelech and the name of his wife Naomi, and the names of his two sons were Mahlon and Chilion. They were Ephrathites from Bethlehem in Judah.

They went into the country of Moab and remained there. But Elimelech, the husband of Naomi, died, and she was left with her two sons. These took Moabite wives; the name of the one was Orpah and the name of the other Ruth. (Ruth 1:1–4)

Ruth was a Moabitess—a foreigner. The Moabites were Israel's oppressors during the judgeship of Ehud (Judg. 3). Israel suffered under the thumb of Eglon, the king of the Moabites, for eighteen years (Judg. 3:12–14). To many in Israel, Ruth was a symbol of an enemy.

In view of this backdrop, the story of Ruth is truly remarkable. It stands to reason that no Israelite would have the slightest reason to help her. Instead, when the book's ancient readers encountered the beginning of the book, they would have expected the people of God to make things harder for her. But Boaz was different. He was a living illustration of how Israel was to bless the foreign nations (Gen. 12:3).

Even more astonishing, Ruth was destined to become the great-grandmother of David (Ruth 4:17–20). Out of the harshest of circumstances—poverty and prejudice and deep-seated wounds of the past—God would raise up the ideal king, whose dynasty would produce the Messiah. If we miss the context of Ruth's story, we miss its most dramatic points of impact.

CHAPTER 42

In the Historical Books, a Person's Tribe and Home Town Are Often Crucial Parts of the Storyline

One of the things I tell people who want to become serious students of the Bible is that they should read the historical narratives in both testaments like they're fiction. Yes, you read that correctly—fiction. I don't say that because I think they *are* fiction. I say that because of the way our minds work when we read fiction, as opposed to a textbook, for example. We instinctively know when reading a novel that a locale, a line, and even a word might pop up later in the story. *We are alert to the fact that the author is doing things to direct our reading.*

That's precisely how we need to read the historical books. They aren't textbooks. Israel's history is presented to us as *story*, and the people who wrote the stories were clever storytellers. The problem is that the hints they drop to lead the reader in one direction or another are often lost on us because we live in another time and place.

One of the best examples is the offensive story of Judges 19, where a certain Levite allowed his concubine to be repeatedly sexually abused. The woman died from the incident, prompting the Levite to exact vengeance. But not until he'd dismembered the woman's body. On the surface, the repulsive episode reminds us that in the time of the judges "everyone did what was right in his own eyes" (Judg. 17:6; 21:25). But there's more to it than that.

To catch the meaning, we need to recall that Judges was written centuries after its events—during the period after the days of Solomon, when the kingdom split in two. The Levite in our story was from "the hill country of Ephraim" (Judg. 19:1)—which readers immediately associated with the heart of the apostate northern kingdom. The Levite is thus cast as a villain from the first verse. The concubine, on the other hand, was from Bethlehem of Judah (Judg. 19:2)—the town of David, the ideal king. The woman had run away to her home and now the Levite had come to Bethlehem to bring her back (Judg. 19:3–9). On the way home, the Levite's servant suggested they spend the night in Jebus—another name for Jerusalem, which would become the city of David (Judg. 19:10). The Levite rejected the idea, since the city was under the control of foreigners (gentiles). Instead, they went to Gibeah (Judg. 19:12ff.). Gibeah was a city in the territory of Benjamin, the tribe of Saul, who was Israel's first king and an enemy to David. It was in Gibeah that the horrible abuse occurred. The men of Gibeah—associated with Saul—are the rapists and killers. The Levite sends pieces of the woman to the rest of the tribes and demands revenge (Judg. 19:29–30). The resulting incident *that closes the book of Judges* is that the tribe of Benjamin is nearly exterminated but is spared.

Ancient Israelite readers would see a victim associated with David suffering at the hands of people associated with Saul. The writer was prepping them for loyalty to David and his line. By the time they read the last line of the book ("There was no king in Israel. Everyone did what was right in his own eyes."), he had them right where he wanted them.

PART 6

LET THE PROPHETIC BOOKS BE WHAT THEY ARE

CHAPTER 43

Most of the Material in the Prophetic Books Isn't About Predicting the Future

In popular usage, Christian or otherwise, the word "prophet" is associated with foretelling the future. That's understandable when it comes to the Bible, since both testaments have prophetic figures making predictive statements about what will come to pass in the future. Despite that truth, it doesn't take long when reading the prophets to discern that most of what they do isn't about predicting anything. More than anything else, prophets were actually preachers. Scholars like to say that a prophet spent more time "forth-telling" than "fore-telling."

What did prophets preach about? Righteousness, mostly. To be more precise, prophets spent most of their ministry railing against the sin and idolatry of the people of Israel and Judah. They were constantly reminding the people of their covenant relationship to God—how they had been rescued from Egypt, delivered at the Red Sea, and given the Law so that they could live happy, productive lives in accord with the God who loved them.

Israel as a nation had publicly proclaimed at Sinai that they would obey God's law (Ex. 24). Prophets were vocal reminders of that promise. In that respect, they were basically covenant enforcers.

They demanded that the people honor their relationship to God. In essence, they were preachers.

It's because of this role that we have the modern expression about "speaking with a prophetic voice." When you hear that phrase, it doesn't concern predicting the future. Rather, the point is that some man or woman is bold enough to tell the truth when it's unpopular or even dangerous. That's what prophets did. And they paid dearly for it.

Modern Bible readers have largely lost the correct orientation for reading the prophets. Talk about the future and discerning "the signs of the times" is more titillating than having someone tell you about your sin. But that's crucial for walking with God. Someone needs to tell the truth. Prophets didn't do it because they enjoyed it. They knew their ministry wasn't going to make them popular. They did it because God wanted to rescue people from judgment.

That alone is a lesson for us today. Most contemporary preaching is about making us feel good about ourselves. There is no warning. It's more important to realize that God loves us and wants us to turn from sin so he can bless us. Our Maker knows that a clear conscience and forgiveness are keys to happiness on earth.

Without a prophetic voice, we deceive ourselves into defining a rewarding life as self-gratification and "looking out for number one." The prophets force us to be honest with ourselves and with God. We can heed their words or reap what we sow. May Scripture awaken us to return to a forgiving God and trusting him with life and salvation.

CHAPTER 44

Prophets Weren't Crazy Men . . . Mostly

One of the themes in the academic study of the prophets is ecstatic behavior of prophetic figures. Prophets fell into trances, convulsed, and participated in otherwise strange conduct. The idea stems in large part from ancient Near Eastern parallels that refer to such figures with vocabulary similar or identical to that found in the Old Testament.

The notion might sound odd, but there is biblical precedent for it. For example, prior to becoming Israel's first king, an episode in Saul's life gives us some insight:

> When [Saul] turned his back to leave Samuel, God gave him another heart. And all these signs came to pass that day. When they came to Gibeah, behold, a group of prophets met him, and the Spirit of God rushed upon him, and he prophesied among them. And when all who knew him previously saw how he prophesied with the prophets, the people said to one another, "What has come over the son of Kish? Is Saul also among the prophets?"

Elsewhere in the Old Testament, the coming of the Spirit on a person enabled superhuman strength (Samson; Judg. 14:6, 19), special wisdom (Isa. 11:2), and visions (Ezek. 37). It was often associated with divine enablement for a specific task, like kingship (1 Sam. 16:13–14) and judgeship (Judg. 3:10; 6:34). The notion of ecstatic behavior, however, more clearly comes from the odd behavior of certain prophets.

Ezekiel is likely the most familiar example of strange prophetic conduct. God told Ezekiel to do several strange things. Ezekiel was told to draw a picture of the city of Jerusalem on a brick tablet and then smash it as a visual aid of how the city would be under siege (Ezek. 4:1–3). God commanded him to lie on his side for 390 days, and then forty more on his right side to symbolically commemorate Judah's punishment in exile (Ezek. 4:4–8). He shaved his head with a sword, then after dividing the hair into three piles, burnt a third, hacked another third with the sword, and scattered the rest into the wind—more performance art about what would happen to Judah and its population (Ezek. 5:1–12). On yet another occasion God told him to publicly dig through a wall and escape through it with the baggage of an exile (Ezek. 12:1–12). If the themes of his behavior hadn't been so disturbing, he'd have been a source of regular entertainment.

Ezekiel isn't the norm, though. Prophecy was mostly about preaching, not unusual abilities to predict the future or performing bizarre and symbolic acts. Some prophets did such things; some did not. In any regard, they were not mentally unbalanced. Whatever God told them to do, or when the Spirit came upon them, there was a point to it. God had a message, and that message needed to be taken seriously.

CHAPTER 45

Old Testament Prophets Preached at Different Times and Places

Since the books of the prophets are grouped together in English Bibles, it appears to most Bible readers that the prophets lived and ministered at roughly the same time. That isn't the case.

The biblical prophets are divisible into two categories. First, there are the prophets who didn't write any books we have in the Old Testament. Some famous prophets like Elijah and Elisha are in that category. They didn't write anything as far as we know. Then there are the "writing prophets," those who left us with material in the Old Testament. The writing prophets are typically categorized into the "major prophets" (the name given to lengthy books like Isaiah, Jeremiah, and Ezekiel) and "minor prophets" (short books like Micah, Habakkuk, and Obadiah).

Regardless of the organizational groupings into which any of the prophets might fall, they lived over a span of hundreds of years. They also ministered in various parts of the promised land.

Most prophetic books contain enough information to situate a prophet chronologically. For example, prophets like Elijah and Elisha lived in the tenth and ninth centuries BC (ca. 950–850 BC). We know that because their ministries overlapped with King Ahab. Isaiah lived in the second half of the eighth century BC since his life intersected with the kings Uzziah, Jotham, Ahaz, and Hezekiah.

Prophets like Jeremiah, who mention the end of the line of the kings of Judah, can be safely situated just before the fall of Judah to Nebuchadnezzar of Babylon (ca. 586 BC).

If a prophet lived prior to 722 BC, the date of the fall of the ten-tribe northern kingdom of Israel, they may have ministered to either Israel or Judah. Solving this question depends in part on whether kings of the north or south are mentioned in their written material. It can also be resolved by mention of a hostile foreign empire, like Assyria (northern kingdom enemy) or Babylon (southern kingdom enemy), or by means of a focus on Israel/Samaria or Judah.

For example, Ezekiel's prophecy opens at the river Chebar in Babylon, allowing us to know he was among the captives taken from Judah. Hosea's book opens with the list of the same kings who reigned during Isaiah's lifetime (Uzziah, Jotham, Ahaz, and Hezekiah). Hosea ministered in to the apostate northern kingdom, since he mentions the threat of Assyria (Hos. 8:8–9) and focuses on the northern kingdom of Israel. Isaiah, on the other hand, focuses on Judah and its environs.

Knowing the time and place of a prophet is important for interpreting in context. But even when certainty isn't possible, the message of loyalty to God is always clear.

CHAPTER 46

Most of the Material in the Prophets Has Already Been Fulfilled

O ne of the things I noticed with great regularity during my teaching career is the overwhelming propensity of Bible readers to assume that much of what is written in the Old Testament prophets is speaking to a time yet future to *us*. Over and over again, whether in class discussion or their written work, students would take phrases about the "return" of Israel or the restoration of temple worship as speaking about end times in relation to their own lives. The opposite is in fact the case. A couple passages illustrate the problem:

> In that day the remnant of Israel and the survivors of the house of Jacob will no more lean on him who struck them, but will lean on the LORD, the Holy One of Israel, in truth. A remnant will return, the remnant of Jacob, to the mighty God. (Isa. 10:20–21)

> And the surviving remnant of the house of Judah shall again take root downward and bear fruit upward. For out of Jerusalem shall go a remnant, and out of Mount Zion a band of survivors. The zeal of the LORD of hosts will do this. (Isa. 37:31–32)

Many students would presume the return and the remnant spoken of here refers to a future regathering of Israel before (or in conjunction with) the return of Jesus. But that reading rips the passages from their context. Isaiah saw the northern kingdom go into captivity and prophesied that the southern kingdom would suffer the same fate. The first passage could therefore speak of the hope of the return of the northern tribes (something Ezekiel later explicitly prophesied; see Ezek. 37:11–28). The remnant language most clearly refers to the people who would be taken to Babylon much later, since Jeremiah and Ezekiel use the same term of the people captured by Babylon. Both prophets feared this remnant would not be allowed to return to the land when the captivity was over if they did not repent (Jer. 42:1–19; 44:1–14; Ezek. 11:13).

We know from Old Testament history that the remnant of Israel *did* return from captivity. Consequently, it makes much more sense—unless something in the passage makes it impossible—to interpret "return and remnant" language in the prophets to be speaking of the exile and return, events that have already come to pass.

There are similar problems with the "Day of the Lord." That phrase should not be assumed to be speaking of end times. It often does, but context must dictate that conclusion. The same is true of language in the prophets about an Israelite return. In every case, context must dictate the meaning of the text, not modern preaching or our interest in prophecy. Context must drive the conclusion that a prophetic statement refers to a time far removed from biblical days. Otherwise, we force biblical passages to say things that simply are not accurate.

CHAPTER 47

The "Servant" of Isaiah Is Both an Individual and the Collective Nation of Israel

We immediately think of the Messiah at the mention of the servant in the book of Isaiah. This is natural, since the one whom the prophet said would be led like a lamb to the slaughter (Isa. 53:7) and have our sins placed upon him (Isa. 53:6) is called God's servant twice (Isa. 52:13; 53:11). But the servant of Isaiah is often *not* an individual messianic figure. In several passages, Israel is that servant.

For example, in Isaiah 41:8 God speaks to "Israel, my servant, Jacob, whom I have chosen." But in the very next chapter, God sends a servant to the nation of Israel (Isa. 42:1, 18–25). Then the prophet moves back to the corporate servant of Israel in the chapters that immediately follow:

> But now hear, O Jacob my servant,
>> Israel whom I have chosen!
> Thus says the LORD who made you,
>> who formed you from the womb and will help you:
> Fear not, O Jacob my servant,
>> Jeshurun whom I have chosen. (Isa. 44:1–2)

> Remember these things, O Jacob,
>> and Israel, for you are my servant;

I formed you; you are my servant. (Isa. 44:21)

For the sake of my servant Jacob,
> and Israel my chosen . . . (Isa. 45:4)

And he said to me, "You are my servant,
> Israel, in whom I will be glorified." (Isa. 49:3)

Oddly enough, the final reference sets up a transition back to the individual servant whom God sends *to* Israel:

And now the LORD says,
> he who formed me from the womb to be his servant,
to bring Jacob back to him. (Isa. 49:5)

Why the back-and-forth? Can't Isaiah make up his mind? There is a good reason both portraits are in Isaiah. Throughout the Old Testament, the nation was represented by a single individual and by language describing a single figure. Israel is called God's son (Ex. 4:22–23). Later, the king of Israel will be called God's son (Ps. 2:7). King David was called God's servant (Ps. 89:3, 20). This royal son of God was of course from the line of David, the line that would produce the Messiah—Jesus, God's Son (John 3:16).

The logic here is that Israel was supposed to be God's offspring (his "son") through Abraham. Israel was supposed to be above all nations since her king was above all kings (Ps. 89:27). Israel failed, and so God had to accomplish his plans himself. He would come as a man to fulfill the role of son, servant, messiah, and king. The "back-and-forth" portraits show us that God knew all along he would have to fulfill his own expectations to redeem humanity.

CHAPTER 48

Messianic Prophecy Was Deliberately Cryptic

Have you ever wondered how the disciples never seemed to understand the things Jesus told them about himself? Think about it. When Jesus told them that it was time for him to go to Jerusalem and die, it angered and scared them (Matt. 17:22–23; Mark 9:30–32). No one replied, "That's right—I read that in the Scriptures." Peter even rebuked Jesus for saying such a thing (Matt. 16:21–23). The truth is that the disciples had little sense of what was going on. Even *after* the resurrection their minds had to be *supernaturally* enabled to get the message (Luke 24:44–45).

We shouldn't be too hard on the disciples. They weren't dumb. Their ignorance was the result of God's deliberate plan to conceal messianic prophecy. Paul talked about the need for that in 1 Corinthians:

> But we speak the hidden wisdom of God in a mystery, which God predestined before the ages for our glory, which none of the rulers of this age knew. For if they had known *it*, they would not have crucified the Lord of glory. (1 Cor. 2:7–8 LEB)

If Satan and the powers of darkness had known that instigating people to kill the Messiah was part of God's design to accomplish

123

their own doom, they never would have done it. The Gospels are clear that Satan and demons knew the prophesied son of David had come (Matt. 8:28–29; Luke 4:31–35). The Old Testament was clear that would happen at some point. But what it concealed was the plan of redemption.

Let's take Isaiah 53 as an example. It's clear that God's servant would suffer for sins, but the Hebrew word translated "messiah" (*mashiach*) never occurs in the passage. It occurs only once in all of Isaiah, and even then it is used of Cyrus, a pagan king. The word does not occur in Jeremiah or Ezekiel and is only found once in the Minor Prophets (Hab. 3:13) where it speaks of the nation. The occurrences in the Psalms refer to Israel's king. Only a handful of them are quoted by New Testament authors of the messianic king, and their application only became clear after Jesus's death and resurrection. Even the label "son of God" isn't helpful since Israel is called God's son in Exodus 4:22–23, and kings like David got that title too.

As shocking as it sounds, there isn't a single verse in the Old Testament that refers to a suffering messiah (*mashiach*) who would be God incarnate, die, and rise again. *That's deliberate.* What we do get in the Old Testament are all the pieces of that profile scattered in dozens, even hundreds of places. *The portrait could only be discerned after the fact.*

The plan of salvation was a cosmic chess game that had to be won. The rest of prophecy unfolds in the same way, in fulfilments hidden in plain sight.

PART 7

LET THE WISDOM BOOKS BE WHAT THEY ARE

CHAPTER 49

Proverbs Are Neither Prophecies nor Promises

B ible interpretation can be a lot like rendering a verdict in a court
  case. A jury has to have the data, the factual material relevant
to the case at hand. It then needs to frame the data in the most
coherent way. The goal is to declare guilt or innocence "beyond a
reasonable doubt," to be convinced that any other interpretation
of the evidence is unreasonable.

Jury decisions can go terribly wrong, however, when some crucial point of data is omitted or overlooked in its deliberation. The
same thing is true for understanding the Bible. A good illustration
is the nature of biblical proverbs.

Proverbs are pithy sayings, or statements that are, by and large,
true in everyday life. The proverb is a well-known literary genre
in all cultures because people in all human cultures want to live
wisely and to get the most out of life. No one expects a proverb to
always be true. That isn't its nature. Likewise, biblical proverbs are
not true in all cases. They are, like all other proverbs, mostly true.
They are truisms.

Because a proverb is a *condensed* piece of wisdom, it cannot
address all the contingencies that could occur with respect to the
circumstance it addresses. By design that isn't its purpose. For
example, consider Proverbs 1:33: "Whoever listens to me will

dwell in security and rest securely from dread and disaster" (LEB). It simply isn't the case that *all* godly people dwell in security and *never* have fears. Even when the righteous trust God with the outcome of an awful expectation or event (e.g., physical violence), they cannot cease being human by suppressing a fear reflex.

Put another way, proverbs do not promise guaranteed outcomes. Proverbs are not designed to tell the *future*. They are designed to describe the *present*.

This is important for correctly understanding a proverb such as Proverbs 22:6: "Train up a child in the way he should go; even when he is old he will not depart from it." This is a classic example of a truism. More often than not a godly, nurturing upbringing will produce a child who wants to know God and follow him. But we all know exceptions. It isn't a proper response to say that the parenting must have gone wrong in some instance since no parent is perfect. Given that reality, there should be no godly children. The retort isn't coherent. Neither is treating a proverb like a prophecy.

CHAPTER 50

The Books of Psalms and Proverbs Were Edited and Assembled in Stages

I noted earlier that there is evidence of editing in biblical books, and how that should be no surprise. Biblical books classified as wisdom literature lend themselves to that sort of thing more naturally than others.

For example, Psalm 72 tells readers matter-of-factly, "The prayers of David, the son of Jesse, are ended." The only problem with that statement is that it isn't true. There are many psalms of David that follow Psalm 72. The superscriptions of several psalms make this quite clear (e.g., Pss. 86; 101; 103; 108; 109; 110; 139; 140).

The statement in Psalm 72 is a classic marker of editorial activity. What we call the book of Psalms is actually five books. Many study Bibles will mark off the books with Roman numerals. "Book III" of the Psalms begins with Psalm 73. That makes it obvious that the comment in Psalm 72:20, the last verse of that psalm, was at one time the end of the psalms—which is what the verse says. As more psalms were collected and added to form Books III, IV, and V, the statement in Psalm 72:20 was rendered invalid yet allowed to remain in the text out of respect for the sacred nature of the material. The endings of Books I, III, and IV all end with a doxology, something to the effect of "blessed be the LORD, Amen and Amen."

Proverbs also bears the marks of incremental collecting and editing. While we tend to think of Solomon as the author of the book, he is actually one of several figures credited with proverbs by the superscriptions within the book. Solomon is specifically credited with Proverbs 1–22, but the book contains material written by Agur son of Jakeh (Prov. 30:1–14) and Lemuel (Prov. 31:1–9). Much of the book is not attributed to anyone specific but labeled simply "words of the wise" (Prov. 22–24). Proverbs 25–29 are also apparently from Solomon but were "transcribed by the men of Hezekiah, king of Judah" (Prov. 25:1), who lived long after Solomon.

These sorts of indicators have two points of importance. First, they ought to make us more alert to the original context of a psalm or proverb. Sometimes a clear association with someone like David or Solomon is possible, allowing us to situate the content in a rough time frame. But in many instances, this isn't obtainable, so we ought not relate that psalm or proverb to a specific person or situation for interpretation. Second, they are visible testimony to how inspiration really worked—over time and through the use of human hands. Knowing that helps us avoid bizarre ideas about how we got the Bible and helps us answer "difficulties" we encounter in the text, like the statement of Psalm 72:20.

CHAPTER 51

Understanding Hebrew Poetry Is Essential for Interpreting Psalms and Proverbs

When you and I encounter the word "poetry" we immediately think of something read, sung, or listened to that *rhymes*. If we studied poetry academically, we'd learn that there's a lot more to poetry as we know it, but rhyming is our most familiar experience of the concept.

Because we think of poetry this way, it's hard for us to see why Psalms, Proverbs, and other portions of the Bible are classified as poetry. Like English, a line of Hebrew poetry is broken down into smaller units called cola. "Mary had a little lamb // its fleece was white as snow" is a complete line made up of two parts (two cola). But that's really where the similarity ends. The fundamental difference in Hebrew poetry and what we think of with respect to that term is that Hebrew poetry doesn't rhyme in *sound*. It rhymes in *thought*.

This concept of "thought rhyming" is called parallelism. In simplest terms, a line of Hebrew poetry (e.g., Ps. 2:4) can begin with a colon ("The one who rules in heaven laughs"), which is followed by another colon that expresses a similar thought ("The Lord scoffs at them"). The relationship between the two cola is the important item for interpretation. The second colon corresponds to the first in some way. The second element advances the thought of the first. There is a symmetrical relationship in the thought expressed.

This "thought rhyming" can be accomplished in a variety of ways. Sometimes colon two is virtually synonymous with colon one. Perhaps only the vocabulary varies. The example from Psalm 2:4 above fits that description. Sometimes a series of cola will build to a climactic conclusion. On other occasions, the second colon expresses the thought of the first in an inverted way. For example, Psalm 1:6 says,

> (colon 1): For the LORD knows the way of the righteous,
> (colon 2): but the way of the wicked will perish.

The two thoughts here are consistent with one another, but they are like two sides of a coin. By definition if the wicked perish, that fate will not befall the righteous.

Grasping the range of possible "thought rhyme" strategies used in Psalms and Proverbs takes time, close reading, and careful thought. Study Bibles and other books help by providing brief introductions to the techniques with examples. Making an effort to learn about parallelism will provide insight into your reading of those books and help you avoid drawing poor conclusions about interpretation.

CHAPTER 52

The Book of Job Is Not Primarily about Suffering

The *satan*" (i.e., "the adversary") in Job is a member of God's divine court, not the devil of the New Testament. When this divine figure reported to God in Job 1, God asked him where he'd been. He reported that he had been "going to and fro on the earth, and from walking up and down on it" (Job 1:7). So his job was to see if people were obedient to God or not. God took the occasion of the report to brag on Job. He asks the *satan*, "Have you considered my servant Job, that there is none like him on the earth, a blameless and upright man, who fears God and turns away from evil?"

The adversary's answer sets the rest of the book in motion and with it the famous suffering of Job. The adversary has an axe to grind and gets uppity. He challenges God's reading of the situation: "Does Job fear God for no reason? Have you not put a hedge around him and his house and all that he has, on every side? You have blessed the work of his hands, and his possessions have increased in the land. But stretch out your hand and touch all that he has, and he will curse you to your face." (Job 1:9–11). In essence, the adversary challenges God's omniscience and authority—God doesn't really know Job, and since he doesn't, he has no right to praise him.

This is a challenge that God cannot let pass. God cannot just destroy the adversary for his arrogance. That would only eliminate the accuser, not answer the challenge. God's reputation needs vindication. *That* is what the book of Job is really about.

The book of Job devotes a lot of space to presenting and evaluating a range of human responses to why Job is suffering and, ultimately, why the righteous suffer. The book doesn't offer a resolution to this last question. The "answer" comes in an appearance of God in the whirlwind. Job sees clearly that he is not God and has to be silent. But consider the book's conclusion. Job did not sin in his suffering. He does not curse God. In other words, his character shows that God was correct and the adversary was wrong. Job is therefore rewarded abundantly by God (Job 42:10–17). Although readers don't get an answer to why the righteous suffer, they know that, at least in this case, it was to vindicate God. He *does* see, and he *is* sovereign. Like Job, we must trust God is good and knows what he is doing.

CHAPTER 53

The Focus of Wisdom Literature Is Character, and the Most Praiseworthy Character Comes from the Fear of the Lord

Most Bible readers who have spent time in the biblical wisdom material (Job, Psalms, Proverbs, Ecclesiastes, Song of Solomon) will not be surprised by the topic statement. So much of what one encounters in these books is oriented to personal life skills across a wide spectrum of areas and experiences. I think it's worth mentioning, though, since we tend to think of wisdom literature like we do the advice column *Dear Abby*. It's more than that.

One of the things that distinguishes biblical wisdom literature from simple advice is inspiration. God is behind what we're reading, and God knows what leads to happiness or regret, failure or success, life or death. Wisdom literature shows us by word and example how to cope with suffering, character flaws, and tragedy. Instead of providing situational suggestions, it tells us the truth about what is virtuous and what is not. It doesn't try to make us feel good about ourselves. It lays out the path of the wise and the path of the fool and doesn't flinch from making sure we know which category we're in.

Since wisdom is a lifelong pursuit, wisdom literature often

finds its context in the home. Parents must guide their children (Prov. 13:22, 24; 22:6) and children must obey their parents (Prov. 1:8–9; 15:5). The marriage bond must be protected from adultery (Prov. 5:1–14; 12:4; 19:14; 31:10–31). The family unit is tasked with passing on principles of morality, virtue, and justice. Children are the beneficiaries (or not) of the cumulative wisdom insights learned from parents. Since the home produces adults with (or without) sound character, it is the foundation of society—industry, relationships, commerce, and leadership. It is a fallacy to assume that the culture of a nation will be virtuous without personal virtue. It's not an exaggeration to say that human stability depends on wisdom.

Foundational to the home are its leaders' relationships to God. A constant focus of wisdom literature is reverence for God, his laws, and his design. Proverbs famously begins,

> The fear of the LORD is the beginning of knowledge;
>> fools despise wisdom and instruction. (Prov. 1:7)

The same thought is echoed in Psalm 34:11–12:

> Come, O children, listen to me;
>> I will teach you the fear of the LORD.
> What man is there who desires life
>> and loves many days, that he may see good?

Job 28:28 reminds us,

> The fear of the LORD, that is wisdom,
>> and to turn away from evil is understanding.

And Ecclesiastes ends with the words, "The end of the matter; all has been heard. Fear God and keep his commandments, for this is the whole duty of man" (Eccl. 12:13).

Wisdom literature gives us a lot to think about, but its orientation is crystal clear. The path to virtue is never personal gratification and focus on the self. A happy, rewarding life is only possible when people have sound character, and the core to motivation in that pursuit is the fear of God.

PART 8

LET THE GOSPELS BE WHAT THEY ARE

CHAPTER 54

The Words "Messiah" and "Christ" Mean the Same Thing

C hristians affirm that Jesus of Nazareth was the Messiah foretold by Israel's prophets in the Old Testament. Some Bible
students might find it startling, then, that the word "Messiah"
occurs only two times in the New Testament (John 1:41; 4:25).
The mystery disappears when we read John 1:41, where Andrew
says to his brother Peter: "We have found the Messiah." The writer,
John the apostle, adds immediately after those words, "which
means Christ." John 4:25 makes the same equation. But is that
just John's opinion?

The answer is no. The Hebrew word translated "messiah" is
mashiach. It is related to a verb, *mashach*, which means "to anoint."
Hebrew *mashiach* therefore means "anointed" or "anointed one."
It is used in the Old Testament to refer to priests (Lev. 4:16; Num.
3:3), kings (1 Sam. 24:6), and, in context, a specially anointed
deliverer (Ps. 2:2; Isa. 61:1).

The New Testament was written in Greek, not Hebrew. The
Greek word translated "Christ" is *christos*. It derives from the verb
chriō, which means "to anoint, or smear." Consequently, Greek
christos ("Christ") means "anointed one" just like Hebrew *mashiach*.

The above explains why the New Testament writers combined
the term *christos* with "Jesus" to produce "Jesus Christ" nearly 140

times (e.g., Matt. 1:1). The reverse order of terms ("Christ Jesus") is found nearly 90 times (e.g., Rom. 1:1).

The reason for the ordering may be cultural. To a gentile, "Jesus Christ" would have created the impression that "Christ" was the last name of Jesus. The word *christos* also sounds like *chrestos*, a fairly common name in the gentile world. By switching from "Jesus Christ" to "Christ Jesus," *christos* essentially becomes a title ("Messiah Jesus"), which would have helped a gentile audience see the significance of the term. Interestingly, "Christ Jesus" is found in *none* of the Gospels, nor is it found in the writings of John. The earliest occurrence is in Acts 24:24, written by Luke, a gentile. All the other occurrences come from the hand of Paul in his letters to gentile churches.

In either case, the theological messaging was the same. The man Jesus of Nazareth is presented as God's prophesied anointed one (Matt. 2:4) who would heal the nations and save humankind from sin.

CHAPTER 55

Biblical Genealogies Are at Times Artificial

Most Bible students would not regard biblical genealogies as very interesting. The assumption is that they are in the Bible to basically accomplish only one thing: give us generational lineages between people. That isn't the case. Genealogies are not always of the same type. Some genealogies are *deliberately* artificial since they seek to convey some specific point of teaching.

Perhaps the best example of a deliberately artificial genealogy is the genealogy of Jesus in Matthew 1. Scholars have long known that Matthew arranges Jesus's genealogy in three groups of fourteen names. Many of the names come from Old Testament genealogical lists for Israelite kings and patriarchs. And that is precisely how the artificial nature of the genealogy is known.

If one compares the genealogy put forth by Matthew with the Old Testament genealogies which contain the names in Jesus's genealogy, it becomes obvious that the time span covered by the three sections of Matthew's genealogy is too great for the generations Matthew lists. We know how old many of the people in Matthew's genealogy were at death, and so the numbers don't add up. But the most transparent result of comparing the genealogies is that Matthew omits names in the Old Testament lists. Luke, who also provides a genealogy for Jesus, does the same thing—and his names don't always match Matthew's.

Our modern mind is quick to think that Matthew made mistakes. That isn't the case. Matthew was telegraphing something by his three-by-fourteen structure.

Hebrew, Greek, and Aramaic used letters in their alphabets for numbers. Other ancient languages do the same. Many scholars believe that the best explanation for Matthew's structuring of Jesus's genealogy is that the number fourteen is the numerical equivalent of the name *David*. In essence, the three groups of fourteen said "David, David, David" and then ended with Jesus, the son of David, the rightful heir to David's throne. Since Matthew spends a great deal of time on validating Jesus's claim to be messiah in his Gospel, this playful way of pointing to David and the messianic son of David makes sense.

Not every genealogy is as interesting as this one, but they often convey important information by their omissions and selectivity. We need to be mindful that ancient writers did things differently than we do. We can't impose our own sense of "accuracy" on ancient texts when literary artistry in the name of making theological statements may be in view.

CHAPTER 56

The Vast Majority of John's Gospel Is Different from Matthew, Mark, and Luke

The four Gospels are the first four books of the New Testament. If you've ever read straight through the New Testament, or read the four Gospels within a relatively short period of time, they'll feel like they all say the same thing. That's in large part true with Matthew, Mark, and Luke. But John is different. But since his book is about Jesus, our mind may not be alert to the fact that most everything in the Gospel of John is unique to it, and much of what's in Matthew, Mark, and Luke doesn't occur in John.

For example, the Gospel of John doesn't have the Sermon on the Mount, parables, and exorcisms. It says nothing about the birth of Jesus, his temptation by the devil, or the Last Supper. There are also differences in vocabulary (e.g., John refers to the "kingdom of God" only twice, whereas other Gospels do that frequently) and chronology (e.g., the cleansing of the temple occurs early in John's Gospel and late in the other three).

Both ancient Christian writers and modern scholars have taken note of the uniqueness of John's content. Some patterns emerge by contrasting what John includes against the other three Gospels. The most significant observation is how John portrays Jesus. Matthew, Mark, and Luke present Jesus as the prophesied son of David, who came to earth to preach about the kingdom of God. On the other hand, John presents Jesus as the Logos (or Word), the preexistent Son of God who boldly asserts "I AM," which is the covenant name of God in the Old Testament. Instead of presenting Jesus as the teacher of the kingdom, John has Jesus teaching people about himself and his divine nature.

The marked differences between John and the first three Gospels are a good object lesson on the importance of not letting our familiarity with biblical content (in this case, Jesus) impede us from a close reading of the Bible. Presuming that we "know what's going on" in a biblical book dulls our senses to the specific goals of the writer. Every biblical author had an agenda. We can't understand what a book or passages is communicating unless we can discern what the author (named or not) has in focus. Having biblical content taught to us is no substitute for going back to the text, no matter how familiar it seems.

CHAPTER 57

Each Gospel Writer Had His Own Agenda

There are four Gospels for a reason. Their existence isn't an accident. The fact that more than one was written suggests that each writer had a slightly different audience in mind. Examining their content validates that hunch.

Unlike other Gospels, the Gospel of Matthew nowhere states a specific purpose or occasion for Matthew's enterprise. Determining Matthew's audience and objective can only be accomplished by careful reading. Matthew references the Old Testament more than the other Gospels, with special interest in messianic themes such as establishing that Jesus was the "son of David" and how his life fulfilled Old Testament prophecies about the Messiah. Matthew uses distinctive phrases from Jewish literature (e.g., "Father in heaven") more than other Gospels. He includes Jewish customs and terms without explaining them to readers (23:5, 27; 15:2; cf. Mark 7:2–4). All of these things and others indicate that Matthew was writing to a Jewish audience to convince them that Jesus was their messiah.

One of the unusual things scholars have noticed about Mark's Gospel is the frequent use (forty-two times) of the Greek adverb *euthus* (often translated "immediately"). Mark constantly presents Jesus as a man of action—getting things done with expediency. Mark omits Jesus's birth and childhood. There is no genealogy.

These things don't matter to Mark's audience. He writes to people more concerned about what Jesus does than who he is—very different from Matthew. These features make Mark's account conform to Roman cultural values. This is especially important because of the way Jesus died—as a criminal by the heinous method of crucifixion. Mark needs to explain why the crucifixion happened to this audience, and so he blends a description of a man they can admire with a defense of the gospel.

Luke tells us at the outset that he is writing to a Greek friend, Theophilus. Luke (*Loukas*) is a Greek name. Luke uses Greek terms not found in the other Gospels. He seeks to reach a Hellenized world, not Jews or Romans, with the Gospel of Jesus. His strategy is a lengthy letter—his Gospel—to Theophilus, that he "might have certainty" concerning what he'd heard about Jesus (Luke 1:1–4).

Lastly, we come to John, the Gospel with the most unique material. John's agenda is nevertheless transparent. His Gospel devotes the most concerted effort to presenting the deity of Jesus Christ. Only in John do we get the seven "I AM" statements of Jesus, a phrase hearkening back to the name of God given in the burning bush. John includes unique statements uttered by Jesus: "I and the Father are one" (10:30); "whoever has seen me has seen the Father" (14:9); "the Father is in me and I am in the Father" (10:38). And John tells us why. He wrote his Gospel so that readers "may believe that Jesus is the Christ, the Son of God," so that they "may have life in his name" (20:31).

CHAPTER 58

The New Testament Writers Used a Bible Translation for Their Work

The Bible of Jesus and the apostles was the Old Testament. The Old Testament was written primarily in Hebrew, the language of ancient Israelites and Jews. Jesus and his disciples probably had some knowledge of Hebrew, but the common language of Judea in the first century was Aramaic. The Hebrew Bible had been translated into Aramaic by Jesus's day. Consequently, odds are high that Jesus and the Twelve would have preached from a Bible in Aramaic—a translation.

Despite the fact that Aramaic Bibles were commonplace and Jews in the Holy Land spoke Aramaic, the New Testament wasn't originally written in Aramaic. Instead, it was written in Greek. The reason was that Judea wasn't the whole world. Aramaic may have been the common tongue in Judea, but the rest of the world spoke Greek.

Fortunately, the Hebrew Old Testament had been translated into Greek a couple centuries before Jesus was born. That Greek translation was called the Septuagint. Since the New Testament writers could communicate with the entire known world in Greek, the New Testament was written in that language. So, for the most part, the Septuagint was used to quote the Old Testament. And because of the Greek orientation to *both* testaments in the earliest days of the church, the Septuagint and the New Testament combined to serve as the Bible of the earliest Christians.

This has ramifications when it comes to reading and understanding the New Testament. For one thing, at times the Septuagint says things that the Hebrew Old Testament (referred to as the Masoretic Text now) does not. The New Testament use of Old Testament verses for articulating theological points at times makes use of these differences. When that's the case, modern study Bibles indicate that in footnotes. Sometimes the differences derive from translation technique. In other instances (e.g., Deut. 32:8–9, 43) the difference comes from the fact that the Hebrew text used to produce the Septuagint differed from what we now regard as the traditional Hebrew (Masoretic) text. Knowing this can resolve apparent contradictions and explain what a New Testament writer saw in a particular Old Testament verse that might seem obscure to us.

The fact that Jesus, the disciples, the New Testament writers, and the earliest Christians used translations ought to encourage us today. If Jesus, Matthew, John, and Paul, for example, can trust a translation to be the word of God, so can we. Fortunately, we have thousands of manuscripts in the original languages of the Bible that scholars can reference to validate or improve translations, not only for English translations but for translations in languages used around the world. Bible translation is never perfect since no translator is omniscient, but it is light years from a haphazard, imprecise discipline. Know that you have the word of God just like Jesus and the disciples did.

CHAPTER 59

Gospel Writers Connect Jesus to the Old Testament in Both Transparent and Roundabout Ways

Since the New Testament begins with the Gospels, and Jesus is the focus of those first four books, we tend to think of Jesus exclusively in New Testament terms. That's too narrow a perspective. The coming of the Messiah, the Son of God, is rooted in the Old Testament, not only in terms of prophecy but also imagery.

We've already talked about the most obvious way the Gospel writers associate Jesus with the Old Testament: calling him the Anointed One ("Christ"). Other transparent correlations extend from that messianic title. The Gospel writers quote specific prophecies about the birthplace of the Messiah (Matt. 2:6; John 7:42; cf. Micah 5:2) and the lineage of the Messiah (Matt. 1:1; cf. 2 Sam. 7:12–16; Ps. 132:11; Isa. 11:1).

Less obvious, but still familiar, connections are made between Jesus and the Old Testament in other ways. When John calls Jesus the "Word," that label is not original to him. The God of Israel appeared to people in the Old Testament as the "Word" (John 1:1, 14; cf. Gen. 15:1–6; Jer. 1:1–9). And the title "Son of Man" had royal messianic meaning (Matt. 26:64; cf. Dan. 7:13–14).

But the Gospel writers tether Jesus to the Old Testament in cleverer, less overt ways. For example, Matthew wants readers to identify Jesus with the nation of Israel. He accomplishes that in his story of Jesus's childhood. After Joseph and Mary had to flee to Egypt to escape Herod, Matthew quotes Hosea 11:1 ("Out of Egypt I have called my son") to recount how they returned to the promised land. But God's son in Hosea 11:1 wasn't the Messiah; it was the nation of Israel. Matthew used the analogy for several reasons, but one of them was that Jesus had appeared on the scene supernaturally, just like Israel appeared as the result of divine intervention with Abraham and Sarah. Israel would later pass through the sea and then journey into the desert where the nation would be tried and tempted (Ex. 14–15; Num. 14:26 ff.). After Jesus was baptized, he was driven into the wilderness to be tempted by Satan (Mark 1:9–13).

Jesus is also cast as a new Moses by the Gospel writers. When Moses was born, Pharaoh had all the infant boys killed (Ex. 1:22–2:10), and Jesus was likewise threatened by Herod (Matt. 2:13–18). Moses went up on a mountain to receive the Law (Ex. 19:3); Jesus ascended a mountain to give his own "law," the Beatitudes of the Sermon on the Mount (Matt. 5:1).

Links back into the Old Testament are strewn throughout the Gospels. They also appear in other parts of the New Testament. Paying careful attention to how writers quote the Old Testament, where Jesus goes, and what he says at a given location will help you see them.

CHAPTER 60

Parables Are Puzzling but Surprisingly Consistent

It's no secret that parables present interpretive problems. A parable is simply a short story that has a double meaning. That is, there's the obvious meaning of the story and then some other more abstract meaning conveyed by the story. The stories Jesus told were very simple, so you'd think both interpretations would be easily discerned. Not really.

Many writers, preachers, and Bible readers have approached the parables for centuries as though they are allegories. In an allegory, all the characters, events, and objects in a story have a specific meaning. But parables really aren't like that. More recent scholarship on the parables rejects that approach since it's artificial and contrary to what you actually read in the Gospels. When Jesus interprets parables for his disciples, he usually zeroes in on one or two teaching points. He doesn't assign meaning to everything or everyone in the parables.

Jesus actually told the disciples why he taught in parables—and therefore tells us. He draws out the reason by quoting Isaiah 6:9–10:

And [Jesus] said to them, "To you has been given the secret of the kingdom of God, but for those outside everything is in parables, so that

'they may indeed see but not perceive,
    and may indeed hear but not understand,
lest they should turn and be forgiven.'" (Mark 4:11–12)

What Jesus said isn't hard to parse. Parables are meant to obscure and reveal the kingdom of God—which is not so much a place as it is the status of being part of God's family and a follower of his good rule. Jesus taught in parables to convey who he was, what God was up to by sending him. Believers would understand. The spiritually blind and hard of heart would not.

As a result, when reading and interpreting parables, our eye needs to be trained to what they tell us about these things—how they reveal the kingdom of God and its King. The elements of the stories that do that are the important ones. Characters and components on the periphery shouldn't be assumed to have meanings or to serve as elaborations on the central idea that we need to figure out. If we stray from what Jesus tells us to see in parables, our unchecked imaginations will have too much influence over our thinking.

PART 9

LET THE BOOK OF ACTS BE WHAT IT IS

CHAPTER 61

The Book of Acts Provides the Context for Many of Paul's Letters

The book of Acts picks up the New Testament story after the resurrection of Jesus. The book opens with the resurrected Christ giving his disciples instructions on spreading the good news of the cross and his resurrection "in Jerusalem and in all Judea and Samaria, and to the end of the earth" (Acts 1:8). Jesus promises to send the Spirit after he ascends, something that happens on the Day of Pentecost (Acts 2:1–13).

The events of Pentecost mark the birth of the early apostolic church in Jerusalem. The book of Acts follows the triumphs and travails of the followers of Jesus, empowered by the Spirit to advance the kingdom of God. The central characters through the first twelve chapters are Stephen, Peter, and James. That changes in Acts 13, when the Jerusalem church sends Paul and Barnabas to preach to the gentiles.

Paul's conversion had been recorded earlier (Acts 9), but Acts 13 changes the focus of the early Jesus-movement to the journeys of Paul. While Acts includes other figures who traveled with Paul (e.g., Barnabas, Silas, John Mark, Luke, Timothy), Paul is the central figure of the book from that point on.

Anyone who reads through Acts will know that Paul traveled widely, preaching the gospel of Israel's Messiah to people of all nations. Acts tells us Paul went on three "missionary journeys" to gentile nations. Acts 13:1–14:28 chronicles the first trek, during which Paul visited places like Antioch, Perga, Pisidian Antioch (which is in Phrygia), Iconium, Lystra, and Derbe. His second journey is the focus of Acts 15:36–18:22. His itinerary included Philippi, Thessalonica, Berea, Athens, Corinth, and Ephesus. His third and final trip, one that ended in Jerusalem with his imprisonment, is described in Acts 18:23–21:14. Paul revisited places he'd previously ventured as well as new locales; Macedonia, Philippi, Troas, Rhodes, Tyre, and Ephesus are among them. Paul spent three years in this last city.

Experts in Paul's life and ministry have been able to determine that these missionary trips spanned roughly ten years. If we restrict ourselves to the churches named in Acts 13–21, Paul started just over a dozen churches. Chances are good he started more since he visited regions during his journeys on which Acts offers no additional details. Many of the churches that are named received letters from Paul, a good number of which we possess in our New Testament. Understanding those letters (referred to as "epistles") requires paying careful attention to Paul's travels in the book of Acts. Every letter Paul wrote was prompted by a specific occasion. Without keeping the original circumstances that led to his correspondences, we'll fail to grasp the meaning of Paul's words in many places.

CHAPTER 62

The Events of Acts 2 Launched the Reversal of What Happened at the Tower of Babel

The incredible events of Pentecost are something with which virtually all Christians are acquainted. As Jesus promised, the Holy Spirit came upon the disciples, enabling them to speak in the languages of the throng of Jews who had come to Jerusalem from every nation. This miracle resulted in thousands of conversions to belief in Jesus as the risen Messiah, which in turn meant that new believers would return to every nation to spread the word. But while all this is familiar, its Old Testament context is habitually overlooked.

Earlier we saw that the events at Babel provided the context for most of what occurred thereafter, from the call of Abraham through the exile. Specifically, Deuteronomy 32:8–9 informed readers that God disinherited the nations when he dispersed them at Babel. Instead, they were put under the dominion of the sons of God, lesser divine beings. This was why God next called Abraham and started his own people, his "portion" as Deuteronomy 32:9 puts it.

The list of disinherited nations is given to us in Genesis 10, the "table" of the known nations at the time. If you were to look at a map of those nations, they would extend from the Persian Gulf (the area of Babylon) in the east to Tarshish (modern day Spain) in the west. At the time of the writing of Genesis 10, Tarshish was the westernmost land mass known.

Moving to Acts 2, the nations at Pentecost also stretch from east to west, this time from the Persian Gulf to Italy. The names can be different at times because the events of Acts occur in the first century AD, thousands of years removed from Babel. If we read the nations listed in Acts 2 in the order they appear, they proceed from the east to the west. When the list hits the Mediterranean, the nations fork north and south and continue westward.

The point should not be missed. Jews from all nations were gathered at Pentecost and would be a new army of missionaries to spread the gospel to the disinherited nations. The reclamation of the nations begins in the regions where the Jews were exiled and proceeds westward, sweeping across the known world. But why does the list in Acts 2 not extend to Spain, the westernmost region included in both Genesis 10 and the punishment of Babel? Because it didn't need to. Paul would finish the job.

The apostle Paul, the apostle to the disinherited gentile nations, understood the symbolism of what happened in Acts. Twice in his letter to the Romans he expressed confidence and urgency about getting to Spain (Acts 15:24, 28). The repatriation of Spain to the true God (Tarshish) had been prophesied by Isaiah (Isa. 66:19). Paul believed it was his destiny to get there and to bring the rest of the gentiles into God's family (Isa. 66:20–23).

CHAPTER 63

The Book of Acts Is Both Prescriptive and Descriptive

One of the most controversial questions concerning the book of Acts is whether it is prescriptive or descriptive. The two options are clear enough. The prescriptive view says that the practices of the early church in the book of Acts are normative. In other words, they should be practiced today. For some this extends to experiences as well. They argue that believers today should be experiencing displays of power like speaking in tongues and healing. The descriptive view argues that Acts simply describes what happened. For this view, there is therefore no requirement to imitate exactly what the early church experienced or did.

It isn't hard to discern that there is truth in both positions. The difficulty is one of *extent*. The book of Acts very obviously *prescribes* things like believers meeting with regularity, prayer, meeting each other's needs, and appointing leaders (both Jews and gentiles). But are we to presume the leadership of the church has apostolic authority? Should we meet in house churches on a daily basis (Acts 5:42)? Should we expect to perform signs and wonders, and if so, are they only to be performed by apostles and those upon whom they have laid hands (Acts 2:43; 6:8; 8:6, 13; 14:3)? In modern times, when wealth is held in ways outside tangible goods, how can we truly have all things in common (Acts 2:44)? It seems clear that these things are, at least to some extent, only *descriptive*.

This question is directly related to apostolic authority. While the book of Acts clearly shows the apostles appointing servant leaders in the church (Acts 6), there is no evidence that the *office* of apostle has continued. There were several kinds of apostles in the New Testament. The Greek word (*apostolos*) simply means "sent one," so it generally refers to individuals sent to help other churches. In cases like these, modern translations at times render the term as "messenger" (2 Cor. 8:23; Phil. 2:25). One specific group of "sent ones" were the Twelve (John 20:24; Acts 6:2; 1 Cor 15:5), those who had been taught by Jesus "beginning from the baptism of John until the day when he was taken up" (Acts 1:22). Paul directly encountered Jesus (Acts 9) and was taught by him personally (Gal. 1:12; 1 Cor. 11:23; 15:3), so he rightly belongs to a second group of people selected by God to minister to gentiles (1 Cor. 15:7–9; Gal. 1:19; 2:9; Acts 13:2–3; 14:4, 14; 15:40; 1 Cor. 9:6; 1 Thess. 2:6). So far as we can see in the New Testament, it was apostles in these two groups that laid hands on people to gift them for service in the power of the Holy Spirit. That gifting included the power to do signs and wonders, which was critical for the early church, whose new message (repeatedly called a "mystery" in the New Testament; e.g., Eph. 3:3–6; Col. 1:26–27) had to be validated as actually coming from God.

Consequently, to argue that everything in Acts is prescriptive requires the continuation of the second group. This group did not continue for the obvious reason that the original apostles were all dead by the end of the first century. While the apostles appointed leaders in the early church (including gentile churches founded by Paul), their status could not be duplicated.

CHAPTER 64

God Never Intended That His People Be Permanently Identified with Ancient Israelite or Jewish Culture

God didn't ordain the culture of patriarchs like Abraham, Isaac, and Jacob. They were part of the ancient Near Eastern world. The law given to Moses presumed *preexisting* cultural values common to this wide geographical region. This is evident in part because the laws of other nations have some overlap with laws in the Torah. This is not to say that Israel had no unique laws or cultural trappings. There was such overlap, but it was tied to faith in the God of Israel, the God of the Bible.

From the call of Abraham forward, God's relationship with Israel hints that God's human family would extend beyond the world of the ancient Near East. God told Abraham, "In you all the families of the earth shall be blessed" (Gen. 12:3). Even though Abraham and Israel were called to be distinct, God knew his salvation plan was bigger than any ethnic or cultural identity. The book of Acts makes this point unmistakable.

Acts 10 records the conversion of Cornelius, a Roman centurion and a gentile. His is the first conversion account of a non-Jew in the New Testament. Peter played a central role in this conversion, but only after God had given him a dramatic vision that would convince him that the gospel of Jesus, Israel's Messiah, was for gentiles as well as Jews (Acts 10:11–15):

> [Peter] saw the heavens opened and something like a great sheet descending, being let down by its four corners upon the earth. In it were all kinds of animals and reptiles and birds of the air. And there came a voice to him: "Rise, Peter; kill and eat." But Peter said, "By no means, Lord; for I have never eaten anything that is common or unclean." And the voice came to him again a second time, "What God has made clean, do not call common."

The dietary laws of the Torah were well known to Peter and, judging by his response to the vision, had been strictly observed throughout his life. The divine command to "kill and eat" unclean animals, and the interpretation of the vision, was an object lesson for Peter. God would direct him to the house of Cornelius later in the chapter (Acts 10:17–33). To his surprise, he was expected. Cornelius had been seeking God (Acts 10:1–8), and God answered by sending an angel to tell him a man named Peter would tell him what he needed to hear. When Cornelius told him about the angel, the vision God had sent him earlier opened his eyes (Acts 10:34–35): "Truly I understand that God shows no partiality, but in every nation anyone who fears him and does what is right is acceptable to him." The result of Peter's visit opened the floodgates to the spread of the gospel to "all nations of the earth" (Gen. 12:3), irrespective of culture.

CHAPTER 65

Gentile Inclusion in the People of God Didn't Mean Hostility toward Jews and Jewish Customs

The book of Acts and the ministry of Paul and his companions inform us that the people of God after the cross were not a new theocracy or a revived Israel on Old Testament terms. The family of God included believers, Jew and gentile. Entrance only required faith in what Jesus accomplished by his death and resurrection.

From antiquity to our own day, however, the non-Jewish nature of the people of God has been misread in negative ways, even to the point of anti-Semitism. It is absurd to think that the New Testament endorses the hatred of the Jewish people. Even after the conference over gentile inclusion in Acts 15, there is no evidence in Acts that Jews were taunted or prevented from preaching the gospel. The opposite was true.

Paul—a Jew (Phil. 3)—addressed this both in word and deed. The gospel, said Paul, was for the Jew first and then the gentile (Rom. 1:16–17). In every place Paul visited on his missionary travels, he went to the synagogue first. If the Jews no longer had a special status, then his pattern seems odd. But Paul longed for the salvation of his countrymen (Rom. 9:1–5).

Paul also expressed appreciation and even devotion to Jewish law and customs. He knew that the law was no substitute for salvation. It couldn't be. Salvation is an unmerited gift (Eph. 2:8–10; Rom. 4:3–25). Nevertheless, he "delighted" in the law in his inner (redeemed) being (Rom. 7:22). Paul circumcised Timothy before taking him along on a missionary tour so as to avoid the young man becoming an obstacle to the Jews that Paul would preach to (Acts 16:3). Upon his return to Jerusalem, Paul visited the temple (Acts 21:26–30), having taken a Nazirite vow of purification (Acts 26:23–36). This makes little sense if Paul believed Israel had been displaced by God—especially when going to the temple was such a perilous thing for him to do.

Rather than setting Israel aside, the New Testament language should be understood in terms of gentile *inclusion*. God included the gentiles into his family; he didn't exclude Jews. Although modern day "replacement theology" primarily focuses on the interpretation of eschatology, it has become a trendy excuse for anti-Semitic attitudes and political disdain for modern Israel. Politics is no aid to biblical understanding and should not become a filter for Scripture.

CHAPTER 66

The Early Church Did Not Practice Communism

Since communism is a socioeconomic theory put forth in the nineteenth century, thinking that the early church practiced communism seems anachronistic. It is. Yet ever since Karl Marx gave the world communism, people have filtered Acts 2:42–45 through his ideas:

> And they devoted themselves to the apostles' teaching and the fellowship, to the breaking of bread and the prayers.... And all who believed were together and had all things in common. And they were selling their possessions and belongings and distributing the proceeds to all, as any had need.

One of Marxism's most famous slogans seems to fit Acts 2 well: "From each according to his ability, to each according to his need." But that takes Marxism and Acts 2 out of context.

Communism advocates several ideas that are foreign to Old and New Testament theology. It abolishes private ownership of property, seeks a classless society, and uses the power of the state to coerce the populace toward fulfillment of both goals. There is no support in Scripture for these extremes. Two of the Ten Commandments presuppose private property and criminalize its theft (Ex. 20:15;

Deut. 5:21). Wealth is the fruit of labor (Prov. 10:4; 13:4). Inherited wealth is also not condemned (Deut. 21:16; Prov. 19:14). Financial inequality is the inevitable result of inequality in ability and giftedness, interest in wealth, a society's opportunities for economic advancement (or lack thereof), and positive versus self-destructive personal decisions (Matt. 25:14–30). While, in Jesus's words, there will always be poor (John 12:8) and therefore unequal economic classes, God doesn't disdain the poor. Instead, he is displeased when they are oppressed by the wealthy (e.g., Deut. 24:14; Prov. 14:31; Zech. 7:10; James 2:6).

Marxist interpreters of Acts 2 miss the obvious fact that everything we read in that passage was *voluntary*. There was no all-powerful (or ecclesiastical authority) state demanding redistribution of income and wealth. In Acts 5 believers were voluntarily selling property and distributing the proceeds among the believers. Even when Ananias and his wife sinned by deceptively withholding part of a property sale, Peter scolded, "And after it was sold, was it not at your disposal?" There is no coercion in this picture.

Acts 2 does not justify Marxist theory for another reason: it would contradict the teaching of Jesus. It was Jesus who spoke of the kingdom of heaven as distinct from the earthly state (Matt. 22:21). When we prefer (or insist) that the state fulfill tasks Jesus gave to us as disciples and servants, we dishonor the principle of his distinction. Care for others is a spiritual duty, not something to be handed off to secular authority.

PART 10

LET THE EPISTLES BE WHAT THEY ARE

CHAPTER 67

Epistles Are Letters

The word "epistle" comes from the Greek word *epistolē*, which means "letter." We typically associate that word with personal correspondence, but a "letter" might refer to all sorts of documents (commercial, legal, governmental, etc.).

The letters we see in the New Testament are both personal and formal. On the one hand, the writers have a personal attachment to the recipients. Paul, for instance, wrote letters to churches he had founded. Peter and James wrote more general letters to groups of believers who were under persecution. Given the fact that some New Testament letters were aimed at audiences scattered about and not in one location (James 1:1) or were shared with other churches (Col. 4:16), New Testament letters also had a formal feel to them. Their content was considered important for believers who had not been the initial addressees.

In our age of instant and scattershot communication, the art of letter writing has largely been lost. A good letter has discernible components and structure. I can remember learning how to write a letter in grade school. My teacher taught us that letters began with a *salutation* (Dear . . .). Instead of getting right to the point, our salutation was supposed to be followed by some sort of light banter to hopefully set the right tone. We might want to include a preview to what the letter was ultimately about. Then came the body of the letter—whose coherence was fostered or undermined by clear or confused paragraphing. When we were bringing things to a close, we were taught to leave the reader a final reminder so that the main purpose of the letter wouldn't get lost. Then we closed with "Sincerely" if formal or "Love" if appropriate and signed our names.

New Testament letters also followed patterns. Most of Paul's letters open with a personal salutation, greeting, and blessing or note of thanksgiving. Here is an example:

> Paul, called by the will of God to be an apostle of Christ
> Jesus. . . . To the church of God that is in Corinth, to those
> sanctified in Christ Jesus. . . . Grace to you and peace from
> God our Father and the Lord Jesus Christ. I give thanks to
> my God always for you because of the grace of God that was
> given you in Christ Jesus. (1 Cor. 1:1–4)

Paul would then launch into the body, which he divided into a teaching section and an exhortation/application section (cf. Eph. 1–3, 4–6). He often closed by sending more personal greetings to friends by name (Rom. 16:3–16).

Knowing what to expect is helpful for those times when the writer breaks the expected conventions. Recognizing the norm helps draw our attention to the exception, which is usually what the writer intended to do.

CHAPTER 68

Paul's Descriptions of the Powers of Darkness Presume a Cosmic Geography

Deuteronomy 32:8–9 informs Bible readers that God put the nations under the authority of the sons of God when he judged them at the Tower of Babel. Deuteronomy 4:19–20, a parallel to the two verses in Deuteronomy 32, reveals the flip side of that judgment-coin—the gods of the nations were allotted to the people God had disinherited. The result was that God took Israel as his own people (Deut. 32:9), but everyone else was under the dominion of lesser gods. These gods would in time become hostile to God and corrupt the nations (Ps. 82). In effect, non-Israelites were enslaved to demonic entities (Deut. 32:17).

The reversal of this situation came with the arrival of Jesus, his work on the cross, and the coming of the Spirit at Pentecost. In the wake of Jesus's resurrection, the birth of the church signified an aggressive advance in the spiritual battle for the kingdom of God, which launched in the public ministry of Jesus, its king.

The epistles presume this spiritual warfare. The nations are under dominion and their people must be liberated by the gospel and brought into God's kingdom. It's easy to tell because of the terms Paul uses to describe the hostile entities that enslaved people. Paul uses the term "demons" only six times, four of which occur in

1 Corinthians 10:20–21, and that passage draws on Deuteronomy 32:17, where the gods of the nations at Babel are called demons (cf. Deut. 4:19–20; 17:3–4; 29:24–26; 32:17).

Paul refers to these demons by a range of other terms: *rulers* (1 Cor. 2:6; Eph. 3:10; 6:12; Col. 1:16), *authorities* (Eph. 3:10; 6:12; Col. 1:16); *thrones* (Col. 1:16); *dominions* (Col. 1:16). All these words have a common denominator: they describe geographical rulership. They are all used elsewhere in the New Testament to signify human beings ruling over specific places. Paul's language is quite consistent with the notion that the earth's nations are under the dominion of sinister divine beings who are hostile to Jesus and the gospel.

The lesson is simple but profound. This world is not our home. It is enslaved by demonic powers who resist surrendering their subjects to the Most High. This was the world of the apostles; it is our world as well. The battle will continue until the "fullness of the gentiles" (Rom. 11:25) is brought into the kingdom, wrenched free from the powers of darkness.

CHAPTER 69

In the New Testament "Israel" Doesn't Always Refer to the Nation or Its People

Earlier, we saw that use of the term "Israel" varied in the Old Testament. Sometimes "Israel" referred to all twelve tribes, and other times it referred to the northern kingdom of ten tribes following the fracturing of the kingdom. The variation in meaning, then, was due to politics and geography.

The New Testament also uses "Israel" in a variety of ways. It doesn't always refer to the promised land, the twelve tribes, or ethnic Jews. But this time the reason is driven by theology.

The birth of the early church in the book of Acts shows us plainly that God's people were never intended to be identified with ethnic Israel forever. Gentiles were destined for inclusion in the people of God (Gen. 12:3). Because of what Jesus did on the cross, the gentiles were included in Israel. The New Testament refers to this blending as a "mystery" (Eph. 3:3–9).

Paul makes this theology explicit in his letter to the Galatians. He begins with the original promise given to Abraham, father of Israel:

Know then that it is those of faith who are the sons of Abraham. And the Scripture, foreseeing that *God would justify the gentiles by faith*, preached the gospel beforehand to Abraham, saying, "In you shall *all the nations be blessed.*" So then, *those who are of faith are blessed along with Abraham*, the man of faith. (Gal. 3:7–9)

Paul moves from this opening to a discussion of the law. He denies the law's saving power and instead holds up faith in Christ, Israel's Messiah, as the way of salvation. Then he closes his argument with language that would startle both the Jewish and gentile unbeliever:

But now that faith has come, we are no longer under a guardian, for in Christ Jesus you are all sons of God, through faith. For as many of you as were baptized into Christ have put on Christ. *There is neither Jew nor Greek*, there is neither slave nor free, there is no male and female, for you are all one in Christ Jesus. And *if you are Christ's, then you are Abraham's offspring, heirs according to promise*. (Gal. 3:25–29)

Paul couldn't be clearer: *if you are Christ's, then you are Abraham's offspring, heirs according to promise*. There is *one* people of God.

CHAPTER 70

The People of God
Are the Temple of God

Presuming they had access to the Scriptures, the Bible of the earliest Christians was the Old Testament. We have the Old Testament today, of course, but we look at it much differently than early Christians did. One reason is that we live at a time far removed from the days of Jesus, whom the early church expected would soon return. Another is that we live on the other side of the catastrophic events of AD 70, the year the Romans destroyed the Jewish temple.

One of the ways this time differential plays out is the way Christians look at Ezekiel 40–48, the fantastic prophecy of a future temple. Since the prophecy appears in the book of Ezekiel, it was written at the time (or shortly thereafter) Israel's first temple, the temple of Solomon, was destroyed in 586 BC. When the Jews returned from exile, they rebuilt the temple. That second temple (with some updating by Herod) was the temple known to Jesus and the apostles. This second temple was the one destroyed in AD 70.

Many Christians today look at Ezekiel 40–48 and believe it prophesies another literal temple that will be rebuilt just before Jesus returns. No New Testament author, however, saw the prophecy that way. There are no direct quotations of Ezekiel's prophecy in the New Testament. That isn't surprising since the temple was still standing in the days of the New Testament writers, at least up until

AD 70. But even after that date there are no direct quotations. In Revelation, a book that most would date well into the 90s, there are allusions to an idealized temple (Rev. 21), but nothing directly deriving from Ezekiel 40–48.

There's a reason for this seemingly odd omission. In New Testament theology, believers are the temple of God. They have replaced the temple. Believers indwelt by the Spirit are now the place sanctified by the sacrificial blood of Jesus where God's presence dwells. This temple was made at the resurrection and not by human hands (Mark 14:58).

Paul is explicit in this regard. In 1 Corinthians 3:16 he writes, "Do you not know that you are God's temple and that God's Spirit dwells in you?" Here Paul speaks to the Corinthians collectively. But in 1 Corinthians 6:19 he applies this same thinking to individual believers: "Do you not know that your body is a temple of the Holy Spirit within you? . . . You were bought with a price. So glorify God in your body." Paul repeatedly emphasized that believers are the place where the presence of God dwells (cf. Rom. 8:9–11; Eph. 2:22; 2 Tim. 1:4).

For early believers, there was no need to worship at the temple—*they were the temple*. This was significant for a people of God that consisted of both Jews and gentiles. Had a temple been essential, gentiles would have been prohibited from worshipping God by the Jews who didn't follow Jesus. The indwelling of the Spirit removed that obstacle.

CHAPTER 71

The New Testament Writers Expected Jesus to Return in Their Lifetime

Many Christians are riveted by the study of biblical prophecy. They energetically study the Bible and look at current events for possible connections. They want to discern "the signs of the times" in earnest expectation of the return of Jesus.

That thinking actually isn't foreign to the New Testament itself. The apostles and early believers expected the Lord's return to be very soon. It was an impending event that they fully expected to see in their lifetime. We know this was the case from a variety of New Testament passages. Some are easy to read over and never notice. Others are transparent.

In regard to the former, consider Hebrews 1:1–2: "Long ago, at many times and in many ways, God spoke to our fathers by the prophets, but *in these last days* he has spoken to us by his Son." The writer of Hebrews believed he was living in the last days—2,000 years ago. The apostle Peter said that Jesus was manifest to him and others "in the last times" (1 Peter 1:20). Peter warned his readers about the threat of self-serving scoffers "in the last days" (2 Peter 3:3). And the events at Pentecost were part of "the last days" (Acts 2:17).

Some passages are even more direct. The apostle John, writing in the book of Revelation, said, "The time is near" (Rev. 1:3; 22:10). The day of the Lord—the day of Christ's return for New Testament believers—was "drawing near" (Heb. 10:25). Some believers even thought they had missed it (2 Thess. 2:1–2)!

Paul taught the Thessalonian believers what to expect leading up to the Lord's return: they needed to be mindful of their walk and faithfulness so as not to be unprepared like unbelievers would (1 Thess. 5). It was sage advice. If we live as though the Lord could return soon, our lives will be pleasing to God and a blessing to ourselves and others, whether it happens soon or not. Jesus himself taught that no one could know the precise day or hour (Matt. 24:36). And since the intent of biblical prophecies associated with the first coming wasn't obvious, we ought not expect to be able to figure things out this next time. In other words, our interest in, and expectancy of, the future shouldn't be distracting us from living as we should in the present.

CHAPTER 72

Paul Had a High View of the Law, but a Higher View of Jesus

Over the course of my teaching career, I've often heard Christians talk about being "free from the law." Usually that referred to the idea that we can't work our way to heaven—that salvation was by grace, through faith in Christ (Eph. 2:8–9). I certainly agree. That's pretty transparent biblical theology. But sometimes the phrase was taken to mean less coherent ideas, like being free from the law essentially meant there were no rules for Christian living. What we did was up to "how the Spirit led" or (worse) whatever the situation called for. Since all our sins were "under the blood," we'd be forgiven for anything we did. Paul anticipated that last idea and forcefully rejected it (Rom. 6:1–2). Christian behavior matters. But is that legalism? Is that placing Christians "under law"?

The question is understandable but, ultimately, incoherent and misguided. We've seen earlier that Paul had a high view of the law—he delighted in it "after the inward man" (Rom. 7:22). He also took a Nazirite vow, as prescribed by the Mosaic Law (Acts 26:23–36). Was Paul inconsistent? Not at all.

"Law" talk among Christians can be brought into sharper focus and a more biblical understanding when we realize that Paul was rejecting the idea that salvation could be *merited* by obeying the law. Paul refers to "the works of the law" eight times. He clearly says that no one can be justified in God's sight by the works of the law (Gal. 2:16; Rom. 3:20, 28). Those who trust in their obedience to law are doomed (Gal. 3:10). Salvation cannot be earned through moral perfection that is achieved by obedience to God's law. Salvation is a gift, available through the death of Christ (Gal. 2:21).

If salvation is granted freely as a gift in response to what Jesus did (Gal. 2:21; 3:2, 5), it is not a thing that is earned or deserved. Yet Paul said that the law was holy, just, and good (Rom. 7:12). Even in the Old Testament, salvation was sealed by faith. Paul used Abraham, the father of Israel, to make this precise point (Gen. 15:6). The law was given to teach people about holiness—the requirement for entering God's presence—and to enable people to live happy, harmonious lives.

The law was indeed holy, just, and good. But the human heart is not (Jer. 17:9). It is not possible for anyone to keep the entire law. Everyone sins, so grace is the only means of salvation (Rom. 3:23–24). Even flawless outward obedience, were it possible, would be inadequate. Jesus's teaching about the law demonstrated that point. Even if someone hasn't committed adultery, for example, the issue runs deeper than the command; it goes to the heart and one's thoughts (Matt. 5:28). No human can meet that standard of moral perfection except Jesus, who fulfilled the Law's demands and became sin for the rest of us (2 Cor. 5:21). This was Paul's message.

CHAPTER 73

The Epistles Are the Antidote to the Idea That the Righteous Invariably Prosper

Perhaps the notion will be foreign to you, but I've met Christians who presume that material wealth and personal success are proof of God's blessing. It doesn't take much thought to realize how unbiblical that proposition is. Many unbelievers are financially prosperous and quite successful. Conversely, many believers have next to nothing. They aren't poor or persecuted because they don't have enough faith or because they haven't sent money to a television ministry. They are poor for a plethora of reasons, some of them quite complex and systemic to their political and cultural situation. But if they are faithful, they are also blessed.

Frankly, the poor and persecuted believers across the world resemble the early church more than believers in the American church. The Epistles don't portray early believers and their fledgling congregations as unusually prosperous, influential, and relatively carefree. It's exactly the opposite.

It is hard to miss the early believer's social status if one spends any time reading the New Testament. Paul started numerous churches. Poverty and personal need was not unusual in them (2 Cor. 8:1–2; Rom. 16:2; Phil. 4:19; Titus 3:14). Paul and the apostles themselves were poor (2 Cor. 6:10; Phil. 4:11–12). James's words indicate that poverty was common (James 2:2–6). The church at Jerusalem—surely loved deeply by God—was notoriously poor, so much so that Paul collected offerings for Jerusalem almost everywhere he went (Acts 2:42–47; 3:6; 1 Cor. 16:1–2; Gal. 2:7–10; cf. Rom. 15:26–28; Acts 24:17).

First century believers also suffered severe persecution. The New Testament is filled with such descriptions. Despite the claims of modern religious hucksters, the apostles suffered, even though they were the very people one might suppose to be the most prosperous if God's blessing leads to a life without hardship. The apostles were beaten (Acts 5:27–42), and the godly were martyred (Acts 7:54–60). Paul suffered with almost unbelievable regularity (Phil. 3:8–10; 2 Cor. 5:21–29). Most of Peter's first epistle is about enduring suffering for faith in Jesus (1 Peter 2:19–23; 3:14–18; 4:1–19; 5:9–10).

Perhaps the most poignant contradiction to the notion that wealth and prosperity defines the blessing of God is Jesus himself. Jesus was homeless and dependent on the support of others (Matt. 8:20; Mark 15:40–41). His torture and crucifixion for crimes he did not commit is the highest example of suffering for believers (1 Peter 2:19–23; 4:1; 5:1).

The message is simple but direct: believers can, do, and will suffer for no just cause. Such suffering is no more a reflection of divine disdain than the suffering of Jesus. And an ultimate blessing and reward awaits those who follow in Jesus's steps.

CHAPTER 74

The Apostles Taught That Unrepentant Christians Openly Living in Sin Should Be Expelled from Local Churches

Many Christians will no doubt be surprised, and perhaps disturbed, by this assertion. Yet it is something taught quite clearly in the Epistles. But from the outset of our brief look at the subject, we must be clear that "church discipline" (as it has come to be called) had restoration of a sinning believer in view, not jaded shunning.

The most obvious instance of this apostolic teaching is found in 1 Corinthians 5:1–5:

> It is actually reported that there is sexual immorality among you, and of a kind that is not tolerated even among pagans, for a man has his father's wife.... I have already pronounced judgment on the one who did such a thing. When you are assembled in the name of the Lord ... you are to deliver this man to Satan for the destruction of the flesh, so that his spirit may be saved in the day of the Lord.

The idea of "delivering to Satan" reflects the ancient worldview that God's people occupied sacred space, and everywhere else was the under the control of evil. Sin belonged outside the believing community, not in it. Though sin leads to self-destruction, the goal was still that the person's soul would be saved and that genuine repentance would come. In this case, there was a good resolution (2 Cor. 7:7–10).

Though this warning by Paul occurs in 1 Corinthians, it is actually his *second* admonition about this problem. In 1 Cor. 5:9 Paul says, "I wrote to you in my letter not to associate with sexually immoral people." Paul had written an earlier letter to the Corinthians that has been lost.

This "double warning" is actually part of a significant pattern in the New Testament. We see it elsewhere in passages relating to sin problems in churches. In his letter to Titus, Paul said, "As for a person who stirs up division, after warning him once and then twice, have nothing more to do with him" (Titus 3:10). In his first letter to the Thessalonians, Paul admonished believers who were "idle" (1 Thess. 5:14). By the time of his second epistle to the Thessalonians, the problem had not been resolved. Believers who could work to meet their own needs were still mooching off others in the church. Paul gave a second warning and an ultimatum (2 Thess. 3:6–10):

> Now we command you, brothers, in the name of our Lord Jesus Christ, that you keep away from any brother who is walking in idleness. . . . For even when we were with you, we would give you this command: If anyone is not willing to work, let him not eat.

Church discipline was not conducted flippantly. It was for the good of all concerned. Believers in sin won't repent if no one tells the truth about their conduct.

CHAPTER 75

The Apostles Didn't Tolerate Aberrant Teaching about the Gospel

Both testaments of the Bible bear witness to the problem of competing religious ideas that were contrary to biblical faith and theology. In the Old Testament period, the polytheistic religious systems of the surrounding nations were a persistent threat to Israel's exclusive loyalty to Yahweh as the true God. That loyalty was the core of Israel's faith (Deut. 6:4) and the basis for salvation in the Old Testament.

In the New Testament period, idolatry and the danger of worshipping a lesser god was still a target of apostolic teaching and writing. Paul admonished the Corinthians to be careful about eating meat sacrificed to idols, warning them that in doing so they were at risk of committing idolatry and fellowshipping with demons (1 Cor. 10:14–22). Since Paul elsewhere permits eating such meat (1 Cor. 8:4, 7–9), advising believers to not make a fuss about offerings that were sold in the marketplace (1 Cor. 10:25), the issue for Paul must have been avoiding any sort of activity that either was participation in the ritual or could be construed that way.

The greater problem of false teaching, however, seems to involve teachers that professed to follow Jesus but whose teachings altered the simplicity of the gospel—that salvation was only by grace through faith (Eph. 2:8–9) and was available to Jews and gentiles alike.

Paul and the other apostles repeatedly had to deal with "Judaizers," who argued that gentiles had to conform to certain points of the Mosaic law in order to be in right standing before God. Paul referred to those who taught such things as "the circumcision party" and famously confronted Peter for his failure to oppose their teaching (Gal. 2:11–14). Peter knew better but was afraid to speak against Judaizing at Antioch. Paul referred to his behavior as "hypocrisy" that was "out of step with the gospel" (Gal. 2:13–14). The Judaizing seems to have been focused on circumcision (and therefore Jewish identity) since Paul later accuses the Judaizers themselves of being lawbreakers (Gal. 6:13). The point is that they had focused on outward conformity to Jewish identity and not the heart. They presumed that being Jewish meant superior status with God.

Peter himself would later have a problem with false teaching. He, along with Jude, had to confront self-proclaimed prophets who rejected moral authority (Jude 4, 8–10). These false teachers were apparently professing Christians since they participated in the Lord's Supper (Jude 12). Jude rejected their profession, charging that they didn't have the Holy Spirit (Jude 19).

As the Epistles show us, we shouldn't tolerate teaching that alters the gospel or encourages a life devoid of biblical morals. When it comes to false teaching, tolerance is no virtue.

PART 11

LET THE BOOK OF REVELATION BE WHAT IT IS

CHAPTER 76

Revelation Is Hard to Interpret Because Apocalyptic Prophecy Isn't Designed to Be Clear

Even though there's a lot in the Bible that is difficult to understand, most of it was written for clarity. That isn't the case with Revelation. The last book of the New Testament is a classic example of what scholars call the apocalyptic genre. The Greek name of the book, John's *apokalypsis* ("Apocalypse") makes that clear.

Revelation is just one of many apocalyptic texts that have survived from antiquity. The normative features of apocalyptic literature are well known, and Revelation has them in abundance. Apocalyptic books aim to reveal the future, specifically of the end of human history, in a cryptic fashion. Apocalyptic secrets are heavenly and not of earth. For that reason the genre communicates its message in visions and uses angelic mediators to convey its secrets. John's book derives from visions he saw in heaven (e.g., Rev. 4:1–6; 9:17; 10:8; 12:10; 14:2; 19:11). Angels appear in Revelation over fifty times, and in many cases they give John insight into those heavenly visions (Rev. 1:1; 17:7, 15; 19:9; 22:1, 6). Despite this help, the content of the book is called a *mystery* several times (e.g., Rev. 10:7; 17:5, 7).

Unsurprisingly, the book is riddled with symbolic language: unidentified "elders," spirits, living creatures full of eyes (Rev. 4–5);

scrolls with seals, celestial signs (sun, moon, stars; Rev. 6, 9); angels with trumpets (Rev. 9, 11); a great fiery Abyss from which emerge locusts (Rev. 9); a dragon (Rev. 12); beasts emerging from the sea and the earth (Rev. 13); and the great prostitute (Rev. 17).

Basically all of this imagery comes from the Old Testament. Unfortunately for us, the imagery was symbolic to begin with, and Revelation at times changes the contexts and nature of the images. But our real disadvantage is that we come from another time and culture. While ancient readers would have instantly understood particular symbols, our understanding is anything but intuitive since we don't share their worldview. A deliberately cryptic book therefore becomes even more obtuse. To have any hope of understanding the book, we need to first understand the meaning of the metaphors and symbols in the Old Testament and then read carefully for how John uses the Old Testament.

If that sounds like work, it is. And it gets worse. A lot hinges on discerning when the book was written, which in large part depends on one passage in the book that is difficult to interpret. On top of that, it's unclear whether we should read the book as a chronological sequence of events or as a series of repeating cycles. The choice of reading strategy leads to dramatically different conclusions about the book's meaning. The dismaying truth is that Revelation isn't easy to understand because it wasn't meant to be easy to understand. For that reason, be *very* suspicious of anyone who tells you they've figured it out.

CHAPTER 77

The Date of the Writing
of Revelation Is Important
for Its Interpretation

Most of the books of the New Testament can be dated with reasonable certainty. We know when Peter and Paul lived and died, for example, and their lives can be cross-checked with events in the book of Acts, which in turn can be aligned with Roman history to a large degree. The case of John and Revelation is harder, and the interpretive stakes are higher.

The key question for the date of Revelation is whether it was written before or after AD 70, the year the Jewish temple was destroyed. If Revelation was written before that date, much of the content of the book could be interpreted as *leading* to that cataclysmic event. That would mean most (some would say all) of the prophecies in the book have already been fulfilled. If it was written after AD 70, then the book really can't be viewed that way—the prophecies would be still awaiting fulfillment. That's a huge interpretive gap.

There is no clear reference to the temple being destroyed within the book itself. That suggests that the event had not happened—which would favor a pre–AD 70 date for the book. The other view—that the book was written after AD 70—objects that this is an argument from silence. The debate opens with those basic differences. Then Revelation 11:1–2 comes into play:

Then I was given a measuring rod like a staff, and I was told, "Rise and measure the temple of God and the altar and those who worship there, but do not measure the court outside the temple; leave that out, for it is given over to the nations, and they will trample the holy city for forty-two months."

Do John's words indicate that Jerusalem and its temple were *literally* still standing and under attack? If that's the case, then the city was destroyed in three and one-half years, and the book was written before AD 70. And that, in turn, is a serious reason to think it is *not* pointing to a future beyond our time.

Ironically, the view that sees the prophecies as "literally" future oriented must still interpret this passage symbolically—that Revelation 11:1–2 wasn't about the actual temple a few years before AD 70. That view makes its argument by appealing to other items in the book. For example, it is argued that "Babylon" in the later chapters of the book actually refers to Rome (see Rev 14:8; 16:19; 17:5; 18:2, 10, 21). The basis for this suggestion is that other books in the ancient world that are datable to the late first century AD use the term "Babylon" as code for Rome. If Revelation is using that code, it suggests that the book was written after AD 70. Irenaeus, an important Christian writer from the generation that followed the apostles, wrote that the book was written "toward the end of Domitian's reign" in the late first century AD.

We can't know for sure who's right. That's par for the course for Revelation.

CHAPTER 78

The Book of Revelation Makes Extensive Use of the Old Testament

One of the reasons we shouldn't neglect the Old Testament is because we can't understand the New Testament without it. Every book of the New Testament contains quotations from and allusions to the Old Testament. I'm not talking about merely mentioning stories, although that happens. New Testament writers *articulate theology* using the Old Testament. The book of Revelation is a dramatic case in point.

No other book in the New Testament is as thoroughly saturated with the Old Testament as the book of Revelation. The book draws upon the Old Testament hundreds of times. While certain books were particularly influential (Daniel, Isaiah, Zechariah, Ezekiel), the apostle John essentially considered the entire Old Testament as a source for his book.

The dominant influence of the Old Testament may seem surprising. One reason is that John often does not preface his use of the Old Testament with formulaic phrases like "thus says the Lord" or "as it is written." Instead, John embeds Old Testament material directly into his scenes, visions, and angelic revelations. He presumed his readers would be so literate with respect to Old Testament content that telegraphing when he wove it into his work wasn't necessary.

One of the questions John's use of the Old Testament has generated among scholars is whether he is faithful to the original context of the material he quotes. The question arises from passages like Revelation 5, where John combines creaturely imagery from both Daniel and Ezekiel in his vision of the four beasts (Dan. 7) "full of eyes" (the wheels of Ezek. 1). Is John just "doing his own thing" with the Old Testament?

John doesn't ignore the original meaning of these and the other passages he cites from the Old Testament. He is fully aware of the original contexts. Rather, he applies the Old Testament material (words, phrases, symbols, metaphors, etc.) to new apocalyptic messaging in his own work.

What all this means is that the key to interpreting the Old Testament isn't the newspaper; it's the Old Testament. No one can claim to understand the book of Revelation without a thorough grasp of the Old Testament passages John quotes or alludes to. Those Old Testament passages must first be understood within their own original literary contexts and ancient worldview. Only with that framework in hand is anything John says or describes in the least way comprehensible. The neglect of the Old Testament is one reason why nearly all of what it says is a complete mystery to those who read it.

CHAPTER 79

Figurative Interpretation Takes the Book of Revelation as Seriously as Literal Interpretation

O ver the course of my teaching career one of the biggest misconceptions I've encountered about Bible interpretation is the idea that interpreting what the Bible says symbolically or metaphorically equates to concluding that what you're reading isn't real. This is deeply flawed thinking. But it's nevertheless understandable.

Bible teachers and preachers are fond of saying that the Bible needs to be interpreted literally for it to be taken seriously. Taking something "literally" means you're ruling out *any* type of figurative language. That only makes sense if the biblical authors wanted to be taken that way. Sometimes they didn't. Since they were human, much of what they wrote could have meaning on more than one level. Insisting only on literalism stifles communication.

We use words every day in ways that would be comical or offensive if taken literally, yet we never expect what we say to be denigrated or considered phony. When you say on a hot day, "I was roasting out there today," were you? When you say you're madly in love with your wife, should I presume you're insane for being attracted to her? If your boss is hard-hearted, have you just diagnosed arteriosclerosis? When you tell your neighbor his new car is a sweet ride, will he ask you not to lick it again? We can laugh at these absurdities, but *all* of these statements are meant to be taken seriously. They *all* have meaning that corresponds to reality.

Biblical writers didn't live in an alternate universe where people never used figurative language, metaphors, or symbolic references. All of those things are stock elements of the way language works. Pitting "literalism" and "figurative" against each other in some sort of semantic death match demonstrates poor thinking.

The reason we can understand when to take a statement figuratively or literally is because the world we've experienced informs us how to interpret it. In other words, the cumulative effect of our upbringing, our cultural setting, our experiences, and our worldview wires us in such a way that we intuitively know what is meant. To reject figurative interpretations of the Bible is to deny the biblical writers their humanity. Instead of letting them be the authority for understanding what they wrote, we assume we know better.

Instead of bending the book of Revelation to our own will in the name of literalism, we need to do everything we can to think like the writers did and to read what they wrote through ancient eyes. We need to learn all we can about their culture, worldview, beliefs, and historical times. That takes work. Fortunately, we have an abundance of resources today that can help us with that task.

CHAPTER 80

Revelation Uses Many Biblical Symbols, and They All Have Contexts That Guide How We Interpret Them

Just as nonliteral doesn't mean "not real," biblical symbols aren't invitations to interpret Scripture however you want. Symbols not only have true meanings, but their meanings can be incredibly powerful. The meanings of biblical symbols aren't open to our imagination. They are rooted in their usage in Scripture and informed by the worldview of the original writers and readers. They have clear, knowable contexts that must be observed and followed for interpretation.

So in order to understand a biblical symbol used in Revelation, that symbol can't be given a meaning that would be utterly foreign to the biblical writer and his original readers. The goal of biblical interpretation is to interpret Scripture in its own context, not ours. Bible students are fond of that mantra, but when it comes to interpreting Revelation, it is too quickly forgotten.

Many approach Revelation as though modern times unlock its meaning. The locust plague of Revelation 9 describes military helicopters, the grotesque horsemen must surely be tanks and other armored vehicles. The ten heads on the beast from the sea must be a ten-nation European confederacy. The biblical writers didn't know about helicopters or tanks, and there was no Europe when John wrote the book. *But there were armies and empires.* By taking things in context, and especially noting how John uses the Old Testament, we can discern meaning in symbols that transcends time.

The examples above illustrate what happens when we impose our context on the symbols. We're forced toward the false conclusion that Revelation really *couldn't* be accurately interpreted before modern times and modern warfare. To insist that Revelation only has meaning in our modern context is to assert that it was meaningless before our time.

Imposing our context onto Revelation is interpretively flawed for another reason. Many of the symbols in Revelation have no coherent modern counterpart. What is the modern filter for the twenty-four elders and the living creatures that surround the enthroned lamb in Revelation 5? The golden censer of Revelation 8? The two witnesses of chapter 11? The great prostitute of chapter 17? All of these have secure Old Testament contexts.

When it comes to symbols, we must discern the symbol's background and trace its usage and repurposing throughout the biblical canon. Revelation's original readers could do that. Like us, they could know in broad strokes what John was saying. Pressing meaning beyond that point forces the book into a precision that was never intended.